SPELLING and GRAMMAR

IN A WHOLE LANGUAGE CLASSROOM

LESLEY WING JAN

ASHTON SCHOLASTIC
SYDNEY AUCKLAND NEW YORK TORONTO LONDON

Acknowledgments

Thankyou to the students at Eltham East Primary School for providing me with valuable insight into how they learn about spelling and grammar.

Thankyou to Di Snowball for her valued feedback as I wrote this book.

Wing Jan, Lesley.
    Spelling and grammar in a whole language classroom.
ISBN 0 86896 863 3.
    1. English language—Grammar—Study and teaching (Primary).
    2. English language—Orthography and spelling—Study and teaching
    (Primary). I. Title. (Series: Bookshelf teacher support library).
372.61

Copyright © Lesley Wing Jan, 1991.
First published in 1991 by Ashton Scholastic Pty Limited A.C.N. 000 614 577,
PO Box 579, Gosford 2250. Also in Brisbane, Melbourne, Adelaide, Perth and
Auckland, NZ.

Printed by SRM Production Services Sdn Bhd, Malaysia
Typeset in Goudy.
          1 2 3 4 5 / 9

Introduction

Over the last few years there have been some major developments in the areas of language teaching and learning; the underlying principle being that language is learnt in a holistic context rather than in fragmented parts.

This implementation of a whole language approach towards language teaching and learning has left many teachers with the problem of how to organise their written language programs so that children are still taught the spelling strategies and the structure of our language, without resorting to spelling lists and formal grammar lessons.

As a teacher I recognise the difficulties involved in:
- organising a classroom program
- deciding on the content of the program
- planning suitable activities
- assessing and evaluating children's knowledge and use of spelling and grammar.

I have written this book to help teachers establish a program that will meet the spelling and grammar needs of all children in a functional way and provide the security of a framework in which to work, within the context of whole language. It describes an approach to spelling and grammar and includes practical organisational ideas as well as assessment and evaluation strategies and activities designed to develop children's knowledge about specific aspects of written language.

It is not levelled at a particular grade or developmental stage, as the approach outlined could be adapted and/or modified for any group, grade or individual.

CONTENTS

WHAT WE KNOW
ABOUT SPELLING
AND GRAMMAR

Introduction

In this section the characteristics of spelling and grammar learning are explained and the implications for program planning are examined.

Conventions of writing

Spelling and grammar, along with punctuation, are conventions of written language. These conventions should be dealt with as part of the writing process.

Spelling and grammar have been isolated here for the purpose of aiding teachers' understanding of the function and features of each, so that they can more fully help learners develop as competent writers.

Spelling

Spelling concentrates on the features of individual words in the structure of language and how they are written in conventional form to help convey meaning. When a child incorrectly spells a word we need to talk about the elements that are correct and then present the correct form. We also need to provide the learner with a strategy or strategies to help them with the next attempt. Many misspellings occur when a word is being used for the first time.

Grammar

Grammar is the study of the formation and function of words and their relationships to each other in sentences. It has to do with the patterns and structure of our language which enable all of its users to gain or express meaning. The emphasis on grammar teaching should be on how words can be put together to express meaning. The correct forms of grammar can be modelled both orally and in the written form.

When a young child says, 'Daddy gone work' the adult models the correct form by responding with, 'Yes, Daddy has gone to work'. The correctness of the child's first attempt at oral expression of a thought is not criticised, but the correct, elaborated model is provided in a supportive, meaningful context.

Some children come to school using incorrect or non-standard grammar which may reflect their background and the modelled language at home. It is our task to demonstrate to these children the standard forms and help them modify their language to suit the purpose, audience and situation.

Spelling and grammar possess similar characteristics, as the table in Figure 1.1 indicates.

Figure 1.1	
Spelling	**Grammar**
is relevant in the writing context	is relevant in the oral and written context
has to do with the structure and meaning of individual words in a text	has to do with the structure and patterns of our language used to gain or express meaning
is learnt through use	is learnt through use
needs to be treated as part of the writing process	needs to be treated as part of the oral or writing process
improves with plenty of writing and reading opportunities	improves with plenty of speaking and listening experiences as well as reading and writing opportunities
is a problem solving process	is a problem solving process
the ability to use conventional form is developmental	the ability to use conventional form is developmental
children formulate own spelling rules and generalisations	children formulate own grammatical rules and generalisations
usually newly acquired rules are overgeneralised	usually newly acquired rules are overgeneralised
correct forms need to be modelled	correct forms need to be modelled
reading provides models of spelling	reading provides models of grammar
conventional spelling is the goal	conventional grammar is the goal

Stages in speaking development

While speech and writing are different forms of communication the knowledge and skills of each are acquired as a developmental process.

Oral language appears to evolve in clearly defined stages in which the child experiments with and develops knowledge of the many aspects of oral communication. During this early use of oral language children begin to formulate their understanding of grammar. The following description of oral language acquisition is based on information from Rivalland (1985 p 21).

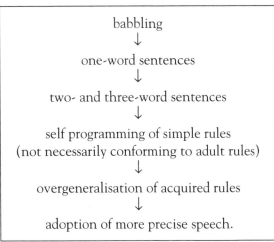

babbling
↓
one-word sentences
↓
two- and three-word sentences
↓
self programming of simple rules
(not necessarily conforming to adult rules)
↓
overgeneralisation of acquired rules
↓
adoption of more precise speech.

Stages of spelling development

Spelling develops in clearly defined stages. These stages have been identified by Gentry (1982), who also maintains that these are systematic and appear to be the child's way of searching for and organising information about our orthography.

It is important to note that children revert to previous stages and strategies when attempting unknown spellings and that one piece of writing may reveal several stages of spelling development. Gentry has described these stages as detailed below.

Precommunicative spelling

This writing, which is the child's first attempts at using symbols to represent writing, is characterised by:

- the random use of symbols which may be conventional or invented
- the inability to be read by others
- the possible repetition of symbols
- the random use of both upper- and lower-case letters.

Semiphonetic spelling

This writing, in which the child attempts to apply letter–sound correspondence, is characterised by:

- the attempt to match each sound with a letter or letters
- the use of one or two letters to represent a word
- the use of letter names to represent the sounds
- a left to right orientation of the letters.

Phonetic spelling

This writing is characterised by:

- the use of children's knowledge of sounds to write words
- the ability to read this writing even though it is not conventional spelling
- the past tense being represented in a variety of ways
- space being left to distinguish between words
- incorrect pronunciation affecting the spelling of words
- nasal consonants perhaps being omitted.

Transitional spelling

The writer is often in this stage for quite a long time and the writing is characterised by:

- the use of other strategies other than the phonetic approach, such as morphemic and visual strategies
- the use of correct letters in words but incorrect sequence
- more frequently used words being spelt correctly
- nasal sounds being included before consonants
- every syllable including a vowel.

Correct spelling

This stage is characterised by:

- the use of all strategies to spell words
- a large number of words being spelt correctly
- the ability to recognise incorrectly spelt words
- the ability to think of alternative ways to spell words
- the use of generalisations to help with new spelling problems
- the effective use of other spelling resources.

Strategies used by competent spellers

Bolton and Snowball (1985 p 11) list the following strategies used by competent spellers:

- the knowledge of the morphological structure of words and the consequent relationships between words (Morphology is the study of the smallest meaningful units of language which are called morphemes. These morphemes can be combined to form new words or may stand alone to create meaning. For example: the word **anybody** is made up of two morphemes, **any** + **body**. The word **unhappy** has the morphenes **un** + **happy**.)
- the knowledge of graphophonic relationships: that is, the variety of sound–symbol relationships, the probability of letter sequences, the likely position of letters in a word and possible letter patterns
- the ability to use visual memory to determine whether a word looks correct
- the ability to develop and use mnemonics, or memory aids

- the ability to use resources such as other people, word lists and dictionaries for a variety of purposes.

It is important that we, as teachers, ensure that these strategies are taught explicitly so that children can apply them to their spelling needs.

Implications for program planning

Program planning must acknowledge the developmental nature of language acquisition. It must cater for the individual rates of learning for the group and be flexible enough to provide appropriate demonstrations and explanations as required.

Correct models of language need to be provided so that children have a clear understanding of what they are working towards. Teachers need sound spelling and grammatical knowledge to be able to intervene as the need arises and help children form generalisations about spelling and grammar so they can understand the function and use of words for different purposes.

Specific grammatical terms, for example, nouns, pronouns or adjectives, may be introduced only after the learner fully understands the function of the words within a text.

In both spelling and grammar teaching, the emphasis must be on the purpose and function of words to express or gain meaning using a written text.

The spelling program would need to include:

- visual memory activities—such as the knowledge of how words should look, or the order of the letters
- morphographic information—the knowledge of the structure of words and their meanings
- resource skills—the ability to use a variety of resources to check for correct spelling
- graphophonic information—the knowledge of sound–symbol relationships.

The grammar program would need to include:
- a focus on the many different forms of writing for different purposes and audiences
- analysis of texts and their structure
- construction of text
- an emphasis on the function of the part in a text.

SPELLING AND GRAMMAR AND WHOLE LANGUAGE

Introduction

This section contains an outline of what whole language means, as well as the characteristics of a whole language program and classroom. It also includes the reasons for this approach to language learning and the implications for spelling and grammar teaching.

What is whole language?

Whole language means:

- all aspects of language—reading, writing, speaking and listening—are interrelated
- each aspect cannot be taught or indeed learnt in separate and isolated parts
- language is learnt in meaningful, functional wholeness and not in fragmented, unrelated parts
- children are empowered by giving them choices as to their language requirements

- responsibility for children's own learning is developed.

So...spelling and grammar are taught within the writing context.

Whole language teachers:

- plan so that the language arises from the subject or content areas being investigated
- build language strategies into their content or subject areas of the curriculum
- observe, intervene and support learners
- make it possible for children to learn about language in real and natural contexts
- have clear expectations as to the direction of children's learning
- take into account children's stages of development, attitudes and needs when planning activities.

So...spelling and grammar are taught within real and natural contexts.

Whole language teachers believe:

- language is easy to learn when it is treated as a whole
- language must be learnt in a purposeful context
- language must be part of all classroom activities
- the more children read, write, listen and speak, the more competent they will become in these areas provided an informed person provides them with appropriate feedback
- language is the tool used to investigate, explore, express, record and compare aspects of the topic being studied.

So...spelling and grammar become part of all written activities within the room.

Whole language teaching ensures:

- language is used purposefully
- children learn about the topic as well as learn how language can be used
- children are empowered to effectively use language.

So...spelling and grammar learning become purposeful to the user.

A whole language classroom is:

- a stimulating environment in which children are supported in their language learning
- a happy and social place in which children interact to gain the most from all experiences
- a well organised and well planned environment in which children use language and in so doing learn about language.

So...spelling and grammar are used by children to help them learn more about language.

Implications

While spelling and grammar are discussed separately in this book, it is not intended that these aspects would be dealt with as isolated, fragmented parts of the writing process. It is intended that all aspects of written language should be treated as part of the whole process of writing.

They have been separated for the purposes of indicating what strategies need to be developed and how the teacher can plan learning settings that develop these.

It is not envisaged that the timetable would reflect fragmented sessions for these aspects of language. Rather it would indicate a language session and these aspects could be demonstrated, discussed and explored within this.

Writing helps children grapple with spelling, punctuation and grammar problems.

A DUAL APPROACH TO SPELLING AND GRAMMAR

Introduction

This section includes an outline of the two-strand approach to spelling and grammar I use in my classroom.

The first strand is designed to provide children with shared experiences with language from which their knowledge about language and its uses can be developed. This is based on 'focus studies' which involve specific demonstration and modelling of spelling and/or grammar conventions often derived from the content areas. This strand also has the purpose of challenging children to explore our written language possibilities through the setting up of specific tasks and activities.

The second strand is designed to provide individual assistance with spelling and grammar as required within the children's own writing and to cater for their particular stage of development and needs at the time.

Reasons for a dual approach

This two-strand approach to written language enables:
- the use of meaningful language activities from the content areas to give children a real purpose for writing, reading and speaking

- children's understanding and knowledge of written language to be developed in a meaningful way through focus studies derived from written language within these content areas
- spelling and grammar to be an integral part of the written language program within the classroom
- children to apply the knowledge they develop from the focus studies to their own individual writing needs
- each child's individual needs to be catered for during their personal writing
- a regular time to be allotted to develop children's awareness of spelling strategies or grammar conventions
- children to: discuss, formulate and confirm their discoveries about conventional spelling and grammar; form generalisations and apply these to their own writing
- program planning that provides for individual and group needs
- children to be responsible for the selection of their own writing needs as revealed in their written work
- the links between reading and writing to be exploited in order to develop children's writing competencies.

Model of a dual approach to spelling and grammar based on focus studies and individual strand

Reading and writing activities derived from topic, theme, subject area.
↓
Focus study or studies derived from the above are planned by the teacher.
↓
Whole class, group or individual attention to focus.
↓
Application of focus to individual writing as required.
↓
Sharing of knowledge gained from these focuses.

Focus studies strand

The focus studies strand is a centring device to narrow children's attention to elements or aspects of spelling and grammar that will aid the development of their knowledge of how our written language works.

The teacher, often through the use of written activities and resources from the content areas, is able to select and provide children with meaningful interactions that draw their attention to texts so they are able to discover, classify and organise their knowledge about our written language. These focus studies are planned interactions with language.

Sources used for focuses

The following samples of writing provide models for spelling and grammar and can be used to focus children's attention on particular aspects.

Children's own writing

Both children's personal writing and the writing related to all areas of the curriculum can provide information on children's needs, and focuses can be drawn from this writing.

Commercially published texts

Published texts (shared books, Big Books) can provide examples of how the conventions of written language are used and these texts can be used for demonstrating specific focuses.

Texts jointly constructed by the class

Any texts constructed in the classroom can provide meaningful contexts for focuses. These texts may be constructed by:

- the teacher in collaboration with the children
- co-operative group work.

The teacher's writing

The teacher may draw out focuses from the following:

- a text the teacher has previously modelled in front of the children
- a planned modelling of a text that will include examples of a chosen focus, for example: plural formations or pronouns.

Environmental print

Signs, labels, directions, instructions and posters provide many opportunities to focus on aspects of our written language.

Lists of theme or topic words

Words related to a theme or topic may be listed and these words may provide specific focuses. The topic words can be sorted according to specific sound–symbol, visual or morphemic criteria.

List of high frequency words

These lists could comprise words most commonly used by children, words in daily use or particular subject terminology.

They can be the basis of focuses and provide further discoveries and generalisations about spelling.

The choice of focuses may be dependent on the particular needs of the individual, group or class of children at the time, the stage of development of children and the relevance of the focus to the children's writing.

Examples of focuses for spelling

These 'focuses' can be of a:

- general nature that children can directly apply to their own individual writing needs, for example: base words, word building, classification activities, or syllabification
- more specific nature that may or may not involve children's individual words but will involve the children in searching printed material for specific information, for example, specific letter patterns or specific sounds.

This list is suggestive only and by no means complete or in any specific order.

Sound–symbol studies
- letter names—*learn the letter names for the alphabet.*
- listening for sounds—*listen for the **o** sound in this text: what letters represent this sound?*
- rhyming activities
  in texts—*provide a word that rhymes with **neigh** in the text.*
  given positions in words—*what letters rhyme with **a** in **eight**?*
- different letters to represent the same sound—***saw**, **door**, **daughter**, **sure**, **store**, **soar**, **paw** represent the **aw** sound.*
- same letters for different sounds—*the letter **a** represents many different sounds: **what**, **water**, **ant**, **ask**.*
- syllabification—*divide words into sections that contain a vowel or a vowel sound: tra\ged\y, fid\dle.*
- substitution of letters in words—***cat—hat—hot—hit—his—him**.*
- homophones—*here\hear, they're\there\their.*
- alliteration activities—*create sentences with all the words beginning with the same sound.*
- silent letters—*lam**b**, **g**nome, **k**nee.*
- classification activities—*group words according to:*
  sound patterns—*words with the **er** sound: w**or**d, b**ir**d, moth**er**, h**ear**d, c**ur**tain.*
  visual patterns grouping—*words with the **ough** letter pattern: en**ough**, c**ough**, th**ough**t, thr**ough**.*
- visual memory activities—*locate words within words: teacher—**tea**, **each**, **ache**.*
- word patterns—*locate words with similar letter patterns or shapes: happy, doll and slipper all have double letters.*

Morphemic knowledge
- word families—***know**, **know**ledge, **know**n, ac**know**ledge.*
- compound words—*break\fast, time\table, fort\night.*
- contractions—*can't (cannot), they're (they are), we'll (we will).*
- abbreviations—*mr (mister), st (street), co (company).*
- base words—*the base word of exploration is explore. The base word of disconnected is connect.*
- word building—*children use a base word and add letters to create new words: swim, swim**ming**, swim**s**, swim**mer**.*
- word origins—*study and explore the origins of words: words that are uniquely Australian-outback such as swagman; words from other countries such as kindergarten (German), restaurant (French).*
- derivations—*study how words are derived from other languages: **tele** is a Greek word meaning distant: many words are derived from this: television, telephone, telescope.*
- affixes—*prefixes or suffixes: **un**happy, wonder**ful**.*
- plural formations—*leaf (leaves), fairy (fairies), donkey (donkeys), child (children).*
- comparatives–superlatives—*happy, happier, happiest; good, better, best.*
- classification activities—*classify words according to:*
  word families—*group words according to common elements: sign, signature, resign.*

open criteria—*group words according to children's own criteria.*
closed criteria—*group words according to directed criteria.*
- formation of tenses—*hope (hope**d**), hop (hop**ped**), pull (pull**ed**)*
- palindromes—*words that are spelt the same way both backwards and forwards: mum, radar, level.*
- eponyms—*words named after people: pavlova, sandwich.*
- homographs—*words with the same spelling but different meanings: I **read** the book; can you **read** the book?*
- anagrams—*words from which another word can be formed using the same letters: felt (left), hops (shop).*
- acronyms—*scuba: **s**elf **c**ontained **u**nderwater **b**reathing **a**pparatus.*
- homophones—*here\hear, they're\their\there.*

Resource skills
- letter names—*learn the names of all the letters in the alphabet.*
- upper- and lower-case letters—*recognise, match and write the upper- and lower-case letters: Ss, Tt.*
- alphabetical order—*arrange letters or words in alphabetical order.*
- use of classroom resources
- dictionary skills—*word location skill: select appropriate definitions and find the relationships between words.*
- thesaurus skills—*word location skill: select appropriate words.*
- use of various directories, atlases—*use a variety of sources.*
- mnemonics—*develop gimmicks to aid the spelling of words: the princi**pal** is your **pal**.*
- classification activities—*classify information according to:*
  type of information—*fact or fiction.*
  organisation of information—*paragraphs, tables of information, labels, graphs, diagrams, charts.*

Examples of focuses for grammar

These focuses are not as clearly defined as for spelling, but are concerned with providing children with information on the functions of words and the relationships between them in sentences.

The following list is not complete and is not arranged in any order.
It is intended to alert teachers to the type of information that can be discussed and modelled as part of the writing process. The terms listed may or may not be used with the children, but the function of parts of sentences should be discussed with them.

- Direct children's attention to the many forms of writing for:
  different purposes
  different audiences.
- Analyse the structure of different writing forms:
  factual writing—reports, explanations
  fiction writing—narratives, poetry.
- Construct simple sentences.
- Create sentences for specific purposes:
  introductory sentences
  lead sentences
  concluding sentences.

- Rework sentences:
  substituting
  deleting
  adding.
- Rearrange parts of sentences to create a more interesting one:
  rearrange words, phrases
  rearrange parts—subject, predicate.
- Create longer, more complex sentences:
  use of conjunctions.
- Add to sentences:
  words
  phrases.
- Note parts of speech and their functions:
  nouns–pronouns, collective nouns, proper nouns, etc
  verbs
  adjectives—comparative, superlative
  adverbs.
- Order in logical sequence to create meaning:
  words
  sentences
  paragraphs.
- Keep correct tense in sentences.
- Use different forms of speech:
  direct, indirect
  first person, third person.

Using the content area for the source of spelling and grammar focuses

My classroom program is based on 'integrated topics' or 'units of work' and I use the content areas as a means of providing demonstrations of the many forms and uses of language. The written language within the topic provides the focuses for word study and for teaching spelling strategies. It also provides opportunities to demonstrate and discuss the grammatical features of our language.

- The topic or subjects to be studied are planned and the written language activities to use with these are selected.
- The written texts to be used or that have been used are collected and studied and the relevant 'focus studies' are drawn out and appropriate activities are planned which should extend the children's understandings of our written language system.
- Resources, activities and materials selected for the topic enable children to be immersed in the language to be used during the unit of work.
- Spelling and grammar become a meaningful part of the written activities within the topic being studied and not a separate activity involving words or skills that may or may not be used or needed by children in their own writing.
- Children see, hear, say and write these words often, which facilitates their development as competent spellers.

- Written language develops naturally from the progression of language activities related to the topic, and spelling becomes an integral part of the writing program.
- As the topic–content area is studied by the children, the classroom can be progressively converted into a stimulating environment of printed material accumulated, collected or made on or about the topic. This printed material can be commercially produced or class–teacher constructed and should represent the variety of written language involved in the topic.
- By 'immersing' children in print it enables them to see the use and importance of spelling in the context of the subject area. It also enables them to be exposed to the structures of the writing appropriate to the topic being studied.

An example of how focus studies can be drawn from printed material related to the unit of work

Select a piece of printed material extracted from the topic being studied as the basis for the focus or focuses. It may be a constructed text, a shared book (or part of a shared book), an individual's writing or a class chart. Ideas for focus activities for spelling and grammar are included in the *Teacher's resource* books for Stages 1–7 of Bookshelf. These relate to each of the children's books in Bookshelf.

Alternatively, construct a text in front of the children which has been planned to include the focus or focuses to be examined. (I have found the use of overhead transparencies an effective way of presenting the written work to children).

For example: *A Day in the life of your body* by Sheila Cubbon (Bookshelf Stage 5) was selected as part of our health topic. The following extract was used to demonstrate explanation writing as well as providing some specific focuses.

While several focuses have been suggested here it is not envisaged that all would be used. They have been listed as examples of the types of focuses that can be drawn from a text. Examine only one focus per session and do not draw too many focuses from the one text.

Spelling focuses

Graphophonic
/o/ sound—How it is represented.

/a/ sound—How it's represented

Visual
'ious'

orphemic refixes

Morphemic Suffixes

Graphophonic Homophones

Morphemic Compound words

While you are asleep, even though your eyes are closed and you are not conscious of information from your senses, your brain is still taking notice of things around and inside your body. Information from your ears still reaches the brain, and you may be woken by a soft noise that is unfamiliar to you but you sleep through a loud noise when you know what is making it. Similarly, you may wake if you get too hot or cold or if there is a light turned on or the sunlight in the morning comes into

Grammar focuses

Writing Form
An explanation

Organisation of information in related sections.

Adjectives

your room. There may also be (chemicals) in the brain that make you drowsy at certain times of day, usually in the evening, and keep you asleep for a few hours.

Visual 'ch'

Rearrange the sentence.

Sleep is a habit and (your) body gets used to the times of day (you) usually fall asleep and wake up. Most of us are used to sleeping at night, but people who have to change to (sleeping) during the day (for instance if they have to (work) at night) can find it difficult to (adjust) for at least a few days. We know that if you are (anxious) or excited, it is difficult to go to sleep and we are not sure how this happens. (Cubbon 1980 p 35.)

Pronouns.

Verbs

Resource Skills
Dictionary work – locate meanings of words.

Resource Skills
Thesaurus work – other words for 'anxious'

For younger children use a wall story, a Big Book or a large copy of a favourite poem or rhyme to help them learn about spelling and/or grammar within a meaningful context. For example: the book *Hands* by Marcia Vaughan (Bookshelf Stage 1) includes a catchy little poem accompanied by colourful and engaging illustrations and photos.

> Hands can open, hands can close.
> Hands can tickle tiny toes.
> Hands can plant, hands can pick.
> Hands can sometimes do a trick.
> Hands can button, hands can zip.
> Hands can help to mend a rip.
> Hands can hug, hands can tug.
> Hands can catch a wriggly bug.
> Hands can feel, hands can peel.
> Hands can grab a wriggly eel.
> Hands can work and hands can play.
> Hands can help you every day.
> Hands can tie and hold a pie.
> Hands can wave to say goodbye.

This book can be used in a variety of ways for different purposes, according to the needs of children. The following activities are suggestions only as to the type of activities that can be planned for specific purposes and are provided as a pattern for other interactions with printed material within classroom programs.

To learn that print carries a message

1 The book can be shared with the children and drama, art, lively discussion can result from the content.
2 The teacher can point to each word and line as the book is read to the children.
3 Read the book several times over a period of time to develop children's understanding that the message doesn't change.
4 Write out pairs of sentences and read these smaller parts to the children.
5 Match the sentences to the illustrations.

To develop the concept of words and letters

1 During shared reading point to each word as it is read. Occasionally pause at a particular word and talk about it. For example, talk about its beginning–middle–end.
   - Count the letters in a particular word.
   - What letter does this word begin with?
   - What sound can you hear at the beginning–middle–end?
2 Point to the words which are repeated or ask children to find words the same as a nominated word.
3 Plan word matching activities.
4 Draw children's attention to letters or sounds that are repeated. They can locate letters that are repeated.

To develop a sense of rhyme

1 Read the poem and the children predict the rhyming words.
2 Read the first line of each pair of lines and children can suggest the last word of the second line.
3 Oral rhyming activities can result. For example:
   - the children suggest other words to rhyme with given words
   - the teacher may suggest alternate lines based on the same pattern and children suggest the rhyming word.
4 A new text can be jointly constructed that uses the pattern. For example:
   - hands can tap, hands can clap,
   - hands can turn the bathroom tap.
5 Build up lists of rhyming words.

A co-operative group searching a text for specific letter patterns.

To develop sound–symbol relationships

1 Ask children the following questions, using selected words in the poem.
   - What letter can you see at the start of **hands/can?**
   - What sound does it represent?
   - Can you see that letter anywhere else?
   - What sound does it represent?
2 The teacher reads part or all of the poem and asks children to listen for particular sounds. For example:
   - clap each time you hear the **t** sound
   - when I say lines two and three, clap when you hear the **k** sound
   - what sound can you hear at the beginning–middle–end of this word?
   - what letter or letters represent this sound?
3 Ask children to find particular letter patterns. For example:
   - find all the words with double letters
   - find the words that end in the letters **ug**
   - find the words that begin with the letter **p**.
4 Alter words to make new words. For example:
   - change one letter to make a new word, **can**—pan, ran, Dan.
5 Make charts using the words from the poem as the focus. For example:
   - words that begin with the letter **h**.

To develop knowledge of the function of words

1 The class makes charts with words that describe hands or words that tell what hands can do.
2 The teacher and children jointly construct an innovated text about feet based on the pattern used in the poem 'Hands'.

Painting the picture

Although there are many possible aspects to focus on in any one piece of writing, limit this to one focus at any session, particularly selecting something that is relevant at the time. The following examples illustrate what could happen.

Scenario one—grammar focus

The class is seated on the floor in front of a copy of a jointly constructed text in report form about dolphins, which was part of the 'sea creature' unit of work. They are reading it with the teacher and editing as required. There is an overuse of the word dolphins in the text, so children's attention is drawn to alternative words that could be used. These are listed on the board as children suggest them and are added to the text to improve its construction, for example: they, their or them. The term 'pronoun' is introduced to the children and they are asked to search other texts around the room to find further pronouns. This has been the focus of the modelling session.

When this modelling session is completed children return to their own writing and reread to check whether they could use pronouns to improve the quality of their texts. Having done this they continue with their writing.

Scenario two—spelling focus

Children are seated on the floor for a further reading of the jointly constructed report and their attention is drawn to the way 'dolphin' is spelt and how the **f** sound is represented in this word. They search the text for words containing the **f** sound, for example, i**f**, o**ff**, li**f**e, cal**f**, enou**gh**, dol**ph**in. These are listed and children's attention is then drawn to the different ways the **f** sound can be represented. These words are then grouped according to their visual pattern and children are encouraged to add to these lists as they find further examples in their reading and writing. For example:

if	off	calf	enough	dolphin
often	sniff	half	cough	elephant
after	offer	shelf	rough	photograph

Children are encouraged to add words to charts around the room.

The children are sent to continue with their own writing. Quite a few are at the proofreading stage and are dealing with the spelling requirements in their writing. Some children are attempting to find the correct spellings in dictionaries, while others are looking around at the charts on the walls to find the correct spelling. A few children are attempting to spell using their have-a-go cards.

A couple of children, who have dealt with all their spelling on their final drafts, are sorting out the words in their word banks that they wish to learn over the next few days.

A small group remains with the teacher for instructions on their activity, which is based on a joint spelling cloze and is the planned focus for this group for the day.

Individual strand for spelling and grammar

The individual strand requires the teacher to be aware of each child's requirements and provide needed assistance as well as encouraging the children to assume responsibility for much of their learning. Children are given plenty of time for writing, both within the unit of work in the form of directed activities, as well as opportunities to choose their own topic, form and purpose. It is through the study of their writing that children's individual spelling and grammatical strengths and requirements can be analysed.

Peer support while writing helps children become more confident to experiment with writing.

Individual strand for spelling

Children are encouraged to **plan** their composition, **write** to get down their ideas, **conference** to share their work and gain audience feedback and then **rewrite** to alter their text until its content is logical and interesting. Before publishing they are required to take care of formal conventions. It is in this proofreading stage that the individual strand towards spelling is developed.

This strand of the program is highly individualised and is designed to help each child deal with their personal spelling needs. It involves establishing a routine so that children learn to proofread effectively and have opportunities to select, group, use, write and learn the words that they have collected from their own writing. Children are encouraged to proofread their work prior to publishing and they may seek the help of peers or the teacher with the task as they further refine this skill. It is at this proofreading stage that the spelling needs of individual children are dealt with and the conventions of our spelling system are emphasised and discussed.

The procedure for the individual strand of spelling

1 When children are at the proofreading stage with their writing, they read it and circle the words if they are unsure of the spelling. Younger children may not be able to proofread their own work, so the teacher will need to perform this activity. As the younger children build up a bank of known words they can proofread these.

After circling the incorrect word they can underline the part of the word that they know is wrong. For example:

2 Some children will attend to all errors in their text while others will only be required to work on a selected number. The teacher needs to assume responsibility for defining the expectations here.
3 Children are encouraged to look around the room for possible sources of required words. For example: topic lists, charts, books.
4 If unsuccessful in locating the word easily within the room, children use their have-a-go cards (see Figure 3.1). They write the word as they think it is spelt and then check with teacher, peer or nominated helper. The child may need a couple of attempts at the word.
5 The teacher should emphasise the correct aspects of children's spelling attempts.
6 If the child, after some help, cannot spell the word correctly the teacher writes the correct form in the third column of the card, while briefly pointing out and discussing features of the word with the child.
7 The child then goes back and using the **look–say–look again–cover–write–check** method (adaptation of Cripps and Peters 1988), writes it correctly in the fourth column. This gives the child

Figure 3.1	**Have-a-go card**		
NAME: Jodie			
DATE: 7/5			
1ST TRY	2ND TRY	CORRECT	CHECK
lin	li _n	lion	lion
trak	tra _k	track	track
harf	ha _f	half	half

Cut this section off when the card is completed and file in student's profile. The third column is cut up for the word bank.

immediate practice at writing the word. It is another opportunity to write the word and develop visual memory.

8 The correct spelling is then written onto the draft.

9 If the child spelt the word correctly at the first attempt on the have-a-go card the correct spelling is written by the child onto the draft and into the child's Words I know book (see Figure 3.2). This is a positive reinforcement of the child's attempts at spelling.

Figure 3.2

10 If the child has circled a word on the draft and this word is found to have been spelt correctly, a tick is placed by the child next to the correct spelling on the draft and the word once again is entered into the Words I know book.

11 During conference times the teacher may select other correctly spelt words from the draft and these are entered into the Words I know book. This procedure is a further celebration of the child's spelling knowledge.

12 When the child has completed a have-a-go card it is date-stamped and the first two columns are cut off and stored in the child's 'language profile' for use by the teacher for evaluation purposes, reporting to parents and teachers or for discussion with the child.
These first two columns provide information on the types of error the child is making and the strategies used to solve these spelling problems.

13 The third column is cut into word strips and these are placed in the word bank for future activities. The final column can be discarded, as it has served the purpose of giving the child immediate practice at writing the learnt word. The words placed in the word banks are the words that children misspelt in their writing.

14 At given times children are required to select and learn some of these words from their word banks. They are encouraged to select words with similar characteristics.

15 Once children have selected the words they wish to learn, they place them in their word wallets so they are easy to locate when they wish to work with them.

Some children may not have many or indeed any words in their word banks. It needs to be established if these children are:

- using an appropriate and extensive vocabulary
- writing a sufficient amount in a variety of forms
- conducting their proofreading properly
- capable, competent spellers
- using all strategies to solve spelling problems.

If they meet the above criteria children should be encouraged and challenged to keep on with their writing and there is no need to worry about the lack of words in their word banks. These children will be provided with challenges and word exploration activities through the focus study aspect of the program.

The observation of the child and analysis of their writing may reveal that they are not competent spellers but are:

- safe spellers
- poor at proofreading
- not sure of the procedures involved.

If children exhibit one or more of the above behaviours the teacher must intervene to help them develop their spelling competencies.

Safe spellers~These children appear to spell correctly all words in their writing, but on closer examination the writing reveals a limited use of vocabulary. Subsequent observation of the child during writing reveals a lack of confidence to attempt new words of which the spelling is unknown. These children may also write very brief texts with little or no inclusion of details which would make the writing more interesting to the reader. The teacher needs to:

- encourage the use of alternative words
- provide oral language activities to build up vocabulary
- model the use of an extensive vocabulary in both oral and written form
- discuss the use of synonyms and antonyms
- praise all attempts at spelling words that are new
- provide spelling games that encourage risk taking
- encourage the child to read as much as possible
- encourage the use of a thesaurus and other resources to provide alternative words
- involve the child in jointly constructing texts
- provide an audience for the writing.

Poor proofreading skills~These children do not have many words in their word banks, but an examination of their writing reveals a lot of words that have not been recognised as incorrect. The teacher needs to:

- praise all attempts to locate errors
- model the proofreading procedure
- emphasise the importance of correct spelling if the writing is to be read by others
- analyse the types of error the child is making and why these are overlooked in the proofreading stage
- provide instruction in specific strategies as required
- help the child proofread their own writing, for example, peer proofreading, teacher assistance while proofreading
- revise the use of the dictionary and other resources to check spelling.

Lack of understanding of the procedure~These children usually have many unfinished drafts and find it difficult to see a piece of writing through to the published form. The teacher needs to:

Figure 3.3

MY LANGUAGE BOOK

My DIARY

WORD PERFECT

The inside back cover has a word pocket. This pocket holds spelling word strips.

- praise all the efforts made to follow the procedure
- revise the steps in the writing process and the reasons for each step
- provide assistance as the child writes: this can be done through more frequent conferencing, providing an audience for the writing and/or jointly constructing a plan of action for the task at hand
- model the writing process
- involve the child in group activities that include the construction of texts.

During conferencing or any written activity, misspellings noticed by the teacher in children's writing can be discussed and the correct form written for the child on a small spelling strip. The child takes the strip and studies the word and then writes it correctly in the text. The word strip is then placed into the word bank for future use. This method is only used when incidental spelling needs arise and it is not expedient for children to use have-a-go cards as the purpose of the activity may be disrupted.

All the books that children use for writing can have book pockets pasted onto the inside back cover and whenever correction takes place in the absence of the child, the correct spelling of selected words can be written on the word strips and placed in the pockets (see Figure 3.3). When children receive the books back they look in the book pockets, take out the word strips, locate the misspelt words in the text and write the correct form. The word strips are then placed in their word banks for future use.

When children have learnt to spell the words, they may request a test by placing their name on a 'request for testing' list or they may choose to leave the words to be partner tested at a later date.

Partner testing procedure

This is conducted regularly and requires that children be instructed in how to do this effectively and efficiently. It is worth taking time to train children so that this activity is a positive learning experience. The following steps are part of the procedure.

1 Children are to divide into pairs.
2 They should sit close together: ideally next to each other to help reduce the noise level as they test each other.
3 Children exchange their personal lists of words that they want tested.
4 One partner acts as the tester for the other.
5 The tester holds the partner's words in the palm of the hand and out of view of the other.
6 The word is said once, put into a sentence and then said once more. Children must learn to do this procedure correctly and not add or repeat any more information.
7 When the word has been written the correct model is placed beneath the partner's attempt. It is not advisable for oral checks to be made, as the children should see the written word.
8 If the word is correct the procedure is repeated with the next word.
9 If the word is incorrect the word strip is put back into the partner's word bank, then the procedure is repeated with the remaining words.
10 When one partner has been tested the roles are reversed and the procedure is repeated.
11 At the conclusion of partner testing both partners record their correctly spelt words in their Words I know books or words I know cards.

Occasionally the tester may not be able to read and/or pronounce or use a word from the partner's personal list, so it is important that the teacher is available to help out when the tester indicates this by the show of a hand in the air. Parental assistance can be valuable during this session.

Partner testing.

The individual strand procedure for use with younger children

The teacher may select from the child's draft the word or words that will be required to be learnt. If possible, it is a good idea to select all words that have a common element. This will help the child's learning. For example: ring, finger, talking.

With younger children a simpler have-a-go card can be made that may also be used in place of word banks. Children attempt the correct spelling as outlined above, but the fourth column is not used at this stage. After the correct model has been written for them, they copy this directly onto the draft.

Children must be instructed to write the whole word and not copy letter by letter. They should not check their copying until they have written the whole word. This is valuable training for visual memory skills.

If the word was correct on the first attempt in the first column, then this word can be written in a simple first letter Words I know book or written on a personal words I know card (see Figure 3.4).

When the teacher needs to quickly provide the correct spelling of a word, it is written directly into the correct model column of the have-a-go card. Because of this the have-a-go sheet needs to be on the child's table during all sessions when writing takes place.

Figure 3.4

My words I know card

NAME: _Christy_____

some school time because		

Periodically children will be required to check their spelling of the words in the correct model column. This column becomes the child's personal spelling list.

Children use a sheet of card that will cover the first three columns of the have-a-go sheet. This can be held in place with a paperclip if necessary (see Figure 3.5).

Figure 3.5

Have-a-go card

NAME: Jodie
DATE:____4/5_____

1ST TRY	2ND TRY	CORRECT	CHECK
			lion ✓
			track ✓
			harf x

The children look at the first word in their list, use whatever strategies they will need to remember the word, cover the first three columns and then using look–say–look again–cover–write–check, they record their spelling of the word.

They uncover the word and check their spelling. If the word is correct they repeat the procedure with the next word. If the word is incorrect they circle it in the correct model column to try again later and then progress to the next word.

At the end of their personal testing they enter the correct words into their Words I know book or words I know card.

Partner testing can be used if appropriate, in which case the have-a-go sheets would be exchanged to provide the list of words. The procedure would then be as detailed earlier.

Individual strand for grammar

As for spelling, this strand is based on the individual needs of the children as they write. This strand runs parallel with the other aspects of the writing process. As the teacher confers with the child, particular grammatical needs can be dealt with using the child's own written language. The teacher can also provide help when individuals reveal poorly developed oral skills.

The procedure for the individual strand for grammar

As children plan for their writing, the teacher can provide assistance by listening to their oral planning and explanation. This will provide opportunities to clarify any obvious oral grammatical errors. As children write their drafts the teacher can discuss individual grammatical needs.

During writing, rereading, conferring with peers or with the teacher, children need to ask themselves the following questions about their writing:

- Does it make sense?
- Does it sound right?
- Is the information arranged so that it is easy to read and understand?
- Has anything been left out that would make this writing easier for a reader to understand?
- Can anything be added to make this writing more interesting?

During the proofreading stage of their writing children can be trained to rearrange sections of their text to improve its quality.

That other strand—incidental teaching and modelling

As with all teaching, regardless of the planning or the strategies used, some of the most effective teaching opportunities arise incidentally. Seize every opportunity to help children use spelling and grammar effectively to become competent language users.

1 When issuing instructions to children, insert adverbs or ask children to provide an appropriate one. For example:
   - give me an adverb to tell me how you are to leave the room
   - tell me how you are to talk to each other
   - give me a word that will tell me how you will write your work.
2 If a notice has to be sent home, draft it in front of the children and talk to yourself as you write so children see how writers write.

3 During morning talk or show and tell sessions, talk about words and their use.

4 During roll call, have children suggest a noun, a verb or a word with **ear** in it instead of the normal response.

5 While reading to children pause occasionally to note the use of words. Be sure this does not detract from the story.

6 During discussions, provide correct models and discuss commonly misused grammar.

7 Songs, chants and poetry provide many opportunities to note spelling and grammar usage.

CLASSROOM ORGANISATION

Introduction

In this section I have attempted to create a picture of the classroom environment that I have found helps children learn about the structure and spelling of our language in a meaningful context. This section also includes suggestions for achieving this environment and the resources required to implement the program.

Painting the picture

The room is not big, but every available space has been used to try and create a lively, colourful and stimulating environment. Seating is arranged in informal groups. The walls are covered with charts, pictures and displays. Suspended from the ceiling are word mobiles, artwork and children's writing.

Trolleys are placed around the perimeter of the room to store children's personal requirements and hold labelled tubs which contain the many requirements for a smoothly run classroom. The tops of these trolleys provide space for permanent or temporary displays. There is a classroom library which includes a range of fiction and non-fiction books. There is a publishing centre where children's work, at varying stages of publishing, is

Charts are set up to help children become aware of the many ways to express meaning.

stored or displayed. Open shelving is provided to enable children to obtain and use all materials and resources with the greatest degree of independence.

A computer is positioned in a corner of the room. Another corner has provision for a tape-recorder and a listening post. A chalkboard and easel are positioned ready for demonstration purposes. Large hooks have been installed beneath the chalkboard and from these hang jointly constructed Big Books, reference charts and large copies of popular poems and chants. A clothes airer is used to hold many of the instructional books compiled by the teacher and children and these books are used frequently throughout the day.

Labelled containers are used to store the resources needed specifically for spelling within the writing process. A small 'poet-tree' has been created, using the frame of an umbrella from which copies of the children's favourite poems are suspended to enable children to read them at any time.

Spelling and word games are stored together within the reach of the children. Portable display boards are placed against bare sections of wall and these are set up, displayed and moved according to the needs of the classroom program.

There is activity at all times as children move between whole class, small group and individual tasks. Each of the children is working on different activities and there is a hum of activity as they interact with each other in purposeful dialogue.

At first the room looks junky and cluttered, but on closer examination, it can be seen that this appearance is carefully constructed to provide the following conditions for literacy learning as outlined by Cambourne (1988):

Peer conferencing: writing for an audience is an authentic reason for checking spelling and grammar.

- **immersion** in print through the use of charts, books, labels, posters, signs and instructions
- **demonstrations** of the many uses of our language through the use of the many forms of written language
- **responsibility** for some of the children's own learning tasks through the provision of work centres, task cards, contracts and the accessibility of resources and materials
- **use** of language through the provision of an environment that creates opportunities for meaningful reading, writing and oral activities
- **response** to children's attempts at language through displays of their work, personal messages and provision of an audience for their work
- **approximation** is encouraged as children use and experiment with language
- **expectation** that children will become competent language users through the implicit and explicit messages given by the teacher
- **engagement** is facilitated by creating this stimulating, organised and supportive classroom environment that challenges and convinces children that these demonstrations of language are within their reach.

Arranging the room

The classroom needs to be organised so that it enables children to be independent workers. For example:

- equipment and resources where children can reach them
- charts displayed where they can be easily read
- the seating needs to be arranged, so that children are able to move easily around the room as well as work co-operatively either in pairs or small groups

- space for children to work individually without interruptions or discomfort
- floor space needs to be provided for whole class, small group or individual activities and an easel or chalkboard needs to be accessible in this area
- interest or activity centres can be set up on trolleys or tables around the room.

Resources needed in the classroom

I have found that the following resources help my written language program proceed smoothly, as well as creating a stimulating environment in which the children become independent workers while developing as competent, enthusiastic and involved language users.

A huge range of printed material for children to read

Correct models of written language, in both commercially produced and class produced books, need to be available for children to read. Some of the printed material that could be provided would include: anthologies, fiction and non-fiction literature, encyclopaedias, comics, magazines, newspapers, cartoons, class made books, signs, labels, posters, directories, picture story books, letters, graffiti boards, and messages.

Our title tally

This chart is filled in by individual children as they publish a piece of written work. It indicates date published, first draft title, published title and name of author. It also includes the style of writing (see Figure 4.1).

Figure 4.1	**Our title tally**			
AUTHOR	WORKING TITLE	PUBLISHED TITLE	FORM	DATE
Darren	Camp	Wilsons Prom. Camp	Rec	2/3
Emma	The Witch	"Bewitched"	Narr.	15/3
Shaun	Basketball	How to Play Basketball	Proc.	18/3
Melissa	Summer	Summer	Poem	29/3

The steps in the writing process

These are displayed around the room and used as a reminder for children on the process of writing. These are constantly referred to during written language sessions and are very important when children are at the proofreading stage of their work.

List of writing forms

This list is used to remind children of the many different forms of writing that can be used for the many different purposes and audiences (see Figure 4.2).

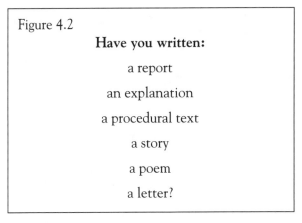

Figure 4.2

Have you written:

a report

an explanation

a procedural text

a story

a poem

a letter?

'Author of the week' board

This board displays the work of a child and is used to celebrate the achievements of individual children. The writing may be in any stage of the process and is used for discussion purposes. A photo and name of the child is included on the board plus the reason for the special reward.

'Look what we've written' board

This display of children's writing is used to explain the writing process and to share children's efforts. Often a particular focus will be selected, for example, the use of interesting adjectives and examples from children's writing are put on display for sharing and discussion.

Lists of possible writing topics

These lists provide suggestions for those children who have trouble selecting a topic (see Figure 4.3).

Figure 4.3

Have you written about:	**Titles looking for authors**
your family	Ouch!
your pets	Lions
school	That was embarrassing!
holidays	How to make...
special events?	Why I like school camps.

Story starter cards

These starter cards suggest characters, settings and situations for a potential written activity. The children are required to select one of each type of card and individually or in groups they construct a narrative to incorporate these (see Figure 4.4).

Figure 4.4

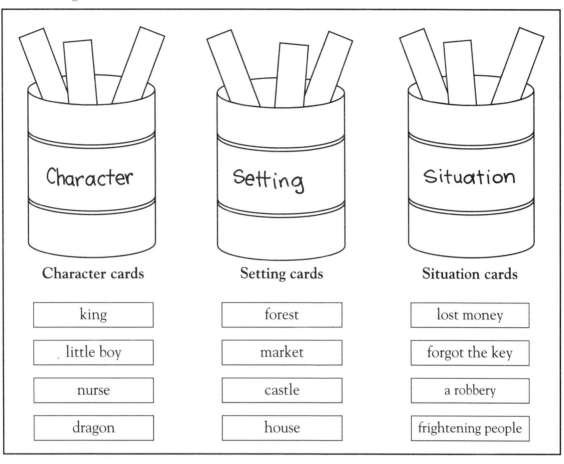

Character	Setting	Situation
Character cards	**Setting cards**	**Situation cards**
king	forest	lost money
little boy	market	forgot the key
nurse	castle	a robbery
dragon	house	frightening people

Use appropriate resources to check spelling.

Figure 4.5 **Topic cards, word tins, word boxes**

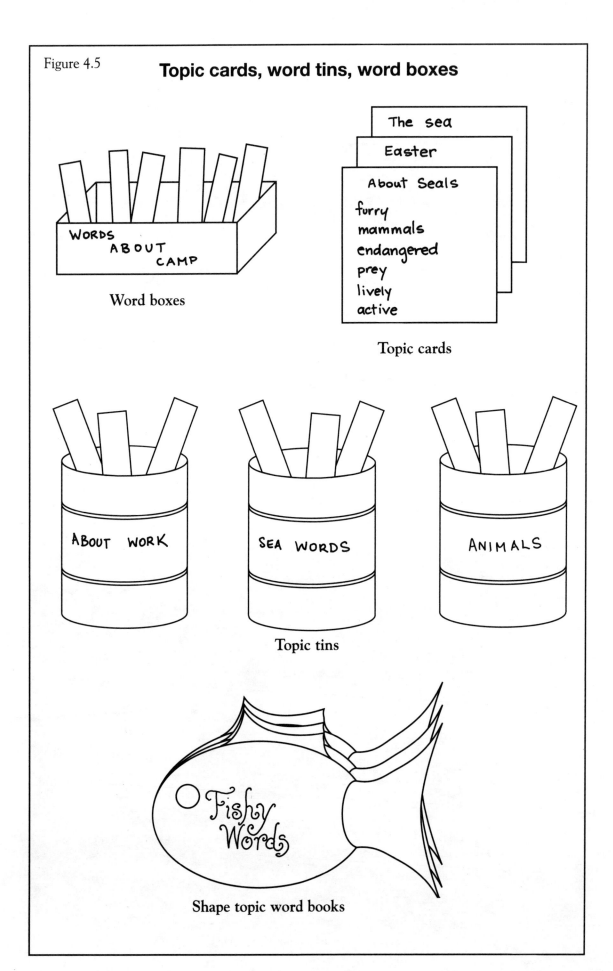

Word boxes

The sea

Easter

About Seals
furry
mammals
endangered
prey
lively
active

Topic cards

ABOUT WORK

SEA WORDS

ANIMALS

Topic tins

Fishy Words

Shape topic word books

A range of commercial dictionaries, thesauruses and spelling aids

These need to be readily accessible and children need to be shown when and how to select and use the appropriate resource.

Topic cards, word tins, word boxes

It helps to use a variety of ways of recording and storing words which enable easy retrieval by the children (see Figure 4.5).

A selection of spelling games

Participation in games is a powerful learning experience and word games help children gain understandings about our spelling system. These can be commercially produced games such as 'Scrabble', 'Boggle', 'Pictionary' and 'Up word' or the games may be teacher or class made such as crosswords, word searches or word dominoes.

'Add-a-bit' board

This board is used periodically to develop children's understandings of how different parts of speech create more interesting written language. For example: the teacher writes a noun and asks children to add as many adjectives or verbs for the given word (see Figure 4.6).

Figure 4.6	**snakes**	
Add adjectives	**Add verbs**
slimy	hiss
scaly	slither
long	slide
scary	hibernate

High-frequency word charts

Words that are to be used frequently are displayed on charts so they can be readily referred to by the children. For example: days, months, colours, maths, science, health terms, 100 most commonly used words, teachers' and childrens' names or local place names.

'How to help me spell' chart

As the children are exposed to ways of working out the appropriate spelling strategies for particular words, these are listed on a chart to help children when they next have a spelling problem to solve.

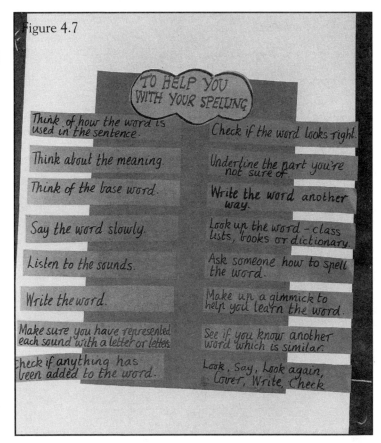

Charts help children organise their thoughts about writing.

'Our spelling demons' chart

Many of the words that children find hard to spell are due to the fact that they haven't seen the words often enough to form a correct visual image of them. The purpose of this chart is to bring to children's attention the most common spelling errors as revealed in the writing of the whole class (see Figure 4.8).

The chart is covered with contact adhesive and the 'demon words' are written on large strips of paper and stuck onto the chart with Blu Tack. They can then be removed easily. Words can be selected from this list as a basis for some of the focus studies.

Figure 4.8

Children are encouraged to add words to the many charts around the room. The more often children see a word, the more likely they are to spell it correctly.

'We can all spell these words' chart

This chart is used as a motivational aid and once again is prepared as for the spelling demons chart. The words on this chart are taken from children's own writing and are words that are spelt correctly by most, if not all of the children.

Periodically (and with adequate warning to the children) some of the words from the spelling demons chart can be checked through partner testing.

We usually make this a fun have-a-go activity in which we 'guess' how many children will be able to spell a particular word. If this number of children can write it correctly the word is transferred to this chart. This 'checking' activity is used to revise and stress spelling strategies as well as to encourage children to have a go at spelling problems.

'We like these words' chart

This chart is used to generate interest in words. It is used to note word patterns, sounds, shapes, silly words, disgusting words, unusual words, long words and short words. The children are encouraged to add their favourite words to this chart. Words are added for many and varied reasons and these reasons can be used as opportunities for discussions about words.

Sound–symbol charts and booklets

These charts can be compiled when a sound–symbol focus has been introduced. Words with a common sound but with varying visual patterns are recorded on these charts. The words are written with the sound pattern underlined (see Figures 4.9 and 4.10). For example:

a chart about words with the **a** sound would include—

lane, **eigh**t, Satur**day**, t**rai**n, p**rey**, **rei**gn, gr**ea**t, caf**e**, g**au**ge.

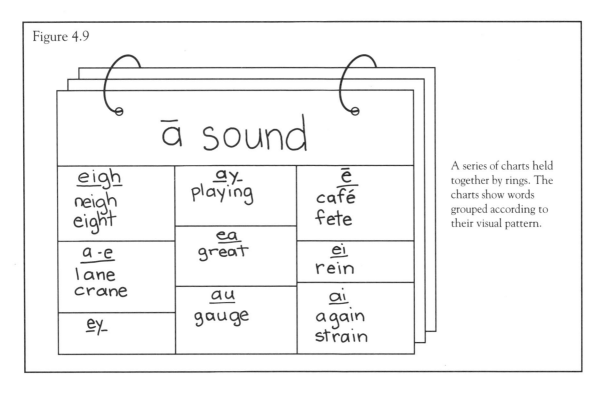

Figure 4.9

ā sound

<u>eigh</u> neigh eight	<u>ay</u> playing	<u>ē</u> café fete
	<u>ea</u> great	<u>ei</u> rein
<u>a-e</u> lane crane		
	<u>au</u> gauge	<u>ai</u> again strain
<u>ey</u>		

A series of charts held together by rings. The charts show words grouped according to their visual pattern.

Same sound—different letters chart. Children group words according to their visual patterns.

Class topic book

This book is used as a class spelling reference and focuses on particular spelling patterns (see Figure 4.11).

As each topic is introduced into the classroom program the words related to the topic are entered into this book under the relevant topic heading. The words may be recorded in this book before and/or during a topic, or at the conclusion of a topic children may be given the task of compiling the topic page using the class lists around the room.

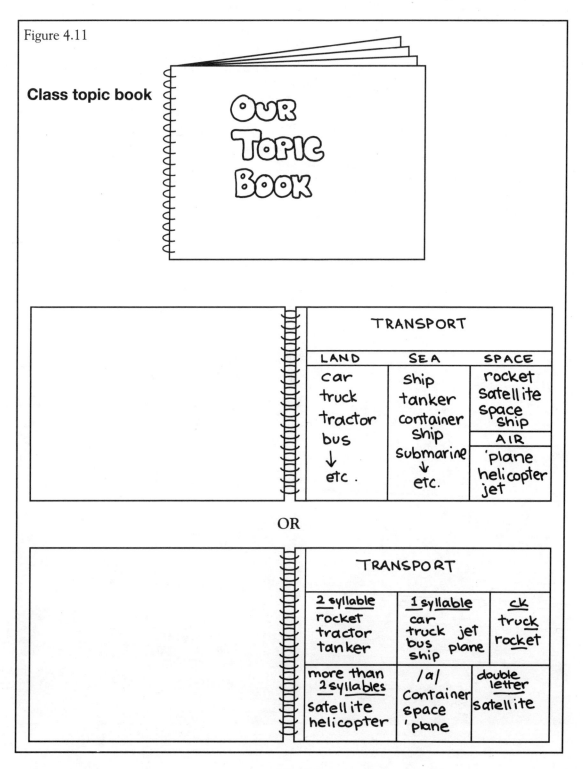

Figure 4.11

Class topic book

OUR TOPIC BOOK

TRANSPORT

LAND	SEA	SPACE
car	ship	rocket
truck	tanker	satellite
tractor	container	space ship
bus	ship	**AIR**
↓	submarine	'plane
etc.	↓	helicopter
	etc.	jet

OR

TRANSPORT

2 syllable	1 syllable	ck
rocket	car	truck
tractor	truck jet	rocket
tanker	bus plane	
	ship	
more than 2 syllables	/a/	double letter
satellite	container	satellite
helicopter	space	
	'plane	

44

Charts around the room challenge children to search for additions.

'Word of the day' chart

This activity is designed to help increase children's word knowledge as well as creating further interest in words. It helps children examine the ways they can learn how to spell words and often the selected word leads onto further discussion (see Figure 4.12).

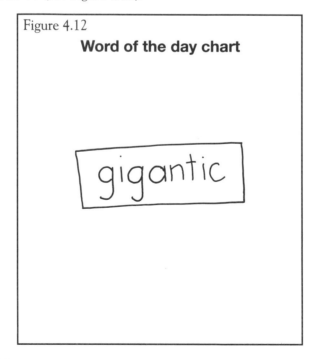

Each child has a turn in sharing with the class an unusual word they have selected. They add the word to the chart and must be able to explain the meaning to the class and why they selected the word.

Handwriting formation charts

Often poor handwriting and poor spelling are linked, so it is important to emphasise the importance of good handwriting as an aid to spelling competency. This chart is referred to as needs arise.

Temporary or occasional charts

These charts are made and used as the need arises and they are not kept as permanent reference charts. For example:

- compilation of lists of current 'focus' words
- topic words charts
- wall stories
- instructions, and graffiti boards.

Alternate words booklets

As a result of discussion, word searching or brainstorming, vocabulary extension books can be made (see Figure 4.13). For example:

- words better than **nice**
- words better than **went**

The contents of these books can be arranged alphabetically (a good activity for children) or arranged under headings.

Figure 4.13

Arrange the words on alphabetical pages.

Grammar focus booklets

It is important to note that parts of speech are functional only within the context of a text and these books are made within this context. They can be made as a result of group work or individual work.

Mix and match books~On strips of cardboard, children write sentences that include specific parts of speech. The sentences are then cut into sections which are collected and assembled into a book that can have the separate sections flipped over to create amusing combinations (see Figures 4.14 and 4.15).

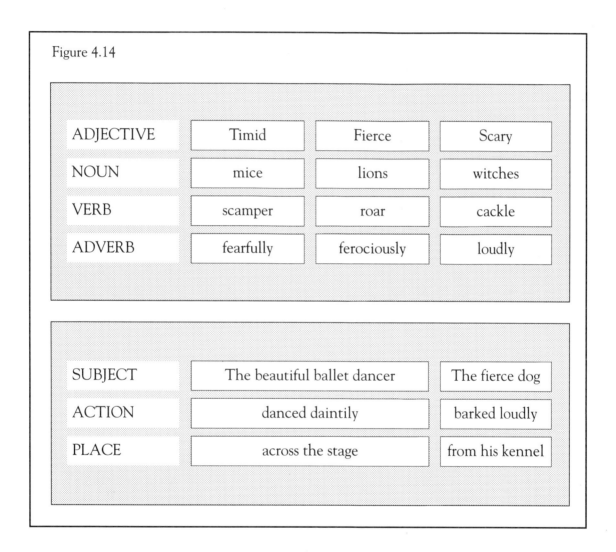

Figure 4.14

ADJECTIVE	Timid	Fierce	Scary
NOUN	mice	lions	witches
VERB	scamper	roar	cackle
ADVERB	fearfully	ferociously	loudly

SUBJECT	The beautiful ballet dancer	The fierce dog
ACTION	danced daintily	barked loudly
PLACE	across the stage	from his kennel

Parts of speech books~As children discover the functions of words they can list them, together with the related sentence, in specific booklets for further reference. The pages in these books can be arranged in alphabetical order. For example:

• Great describing words
• Our book of doing words/verbs.

Also see Figure 4.16.

Collection books~These books contain favourite sentences, phrases or passages. For example: 'Our favourite descriptions of people/places/things'.

Figure 4.15

Our book
of mix and
match verbs,
adjectives, nouns,
and adverbs

MAD
TEACHERS
BARK
SOFTLY

Our book
of mix and
match
Sentences

The fierce dog
danced daintily
from the jungle

Figure 4.16

```
┌─────────────────────────────────┐  ┌─────────────────────────────────┐
│                              V   │  │                              S   │
│                                  │  │                                  │
│  vicious                         │  │  scampered                       │
│  The vicious dog bit the         │  │  scurried                        │
│  postman's leg.                  │  │  The mouse _____         │
│                                  │  │  across the floor.               │
│  vain                            │  │                                  │
│  Eagerly the vain lady waited    │  │  sulked                          │
│  for a compliment.               │  │  scowled                         │
│                                  │  │  She _____ when she            │
│                                  │  │  didn't get her own way.         │
│                                  │  │                                  │
└─────────────────────────────────┘  └─────────────────────────────────┘
```

Topic or theme booklets

These are distinct from the general class topic book as they contain words only from one topic. For example:

- Our book of transport words
- Words about the sea.

Morphemic booklets

As children study the meanings of our words, these can be collected and made into books which then become a further spelling check resource. For example:

- Our book of compound words
- Our word building book
- Our book of tele words.

Sound–symbol booklets

These books are compiled to help children realise that the one sound can be represented by many different symbols. For example:

- Rhyming words
- These words have the **a** sound.

Visual pattern word booklets and charts

These books are compiled to demonstrate to children the many sounds that given letters or groups of letters can represent in words or to focus children's attention on specific letter patterns. For example:

- All about ear words
- Double letter words.

Also see Figure 4.17.

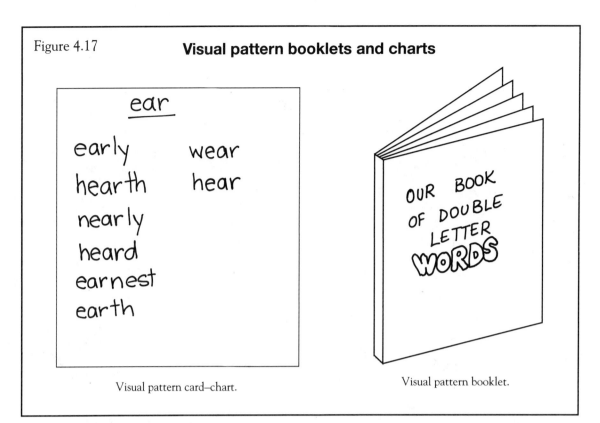

Figure 4.17   **Visual pattern booklets and charts**

ear

early   wear
hearth   hear
nearly
heard
earnest
earth

OUR BOOK OF DOUBLE LETTER WORDS

Visual pattern card–chart.   Visual pattern booklet.

Small blank paper strips

These are approximately 5 cm by 2 cm and are used by the children in their word banks and for compiling word lists for classroom use. They are also used by the teacher to write the correct form of a word when the child's use of have-a-go cards is not expedient enough. For example: an incidental spelling opportunity when spelling is not the main activity of the lesson. These strips need to be in plentiful supply and stored within children's reach. I have found it convenient to have a labelled container of these readily available.

Large blank paper strips

These strips are approximately 10 cm by 4 cm and are used both by the teacher and the children when making or adding words to class charts. These larger strips enable easier reading of charts.

Sentence strips

These are long, narrow strips of paper on which original or copied sentences, phrases or examples of well constructed text can be written and displayed around the room.

These strips encourage the collection of examples and discussion of how our language can be structured to convey meaning.

Resources required by each student

Each child needs access to classroom resources as well as the following individual resources.

Writing folder

This holds the current draft that a particular child is working on and is for daily use. It includes a 'Things I can do' pupil self-evaluation sheet which the children fill out at regular intervals (see Figure 4.18).

Figure 4.18

Writing folder

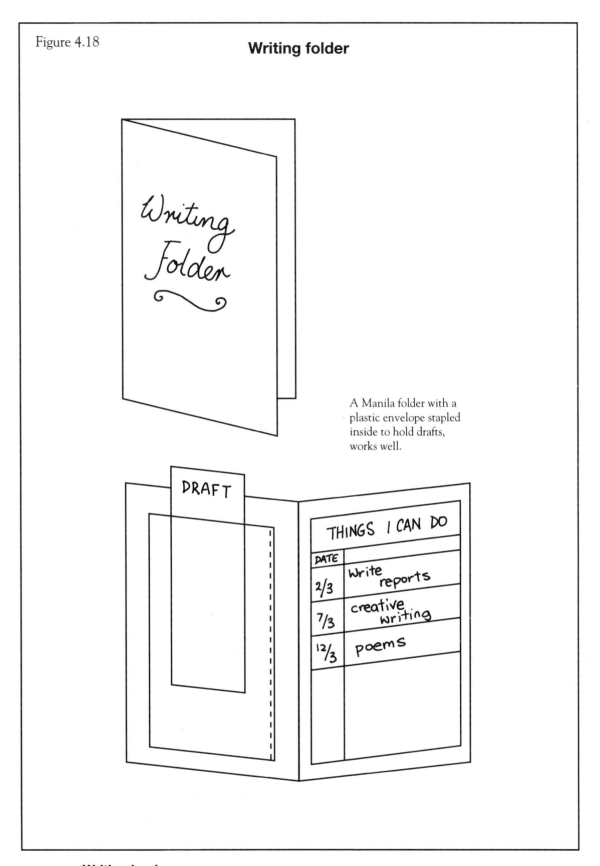

A Manila folder with a plastic envelope stapled inside to hold drafts, works well.

DRAFT

THINGS I CAN DO	
DATE	
2/3	Write reports
7/3	creative writing
12/3	poems

Writing banks

This large folder holds the dated drafts the child has finished with or no longer wishes to work on. The child may come back to work on a draft later (see Figure 4.19).

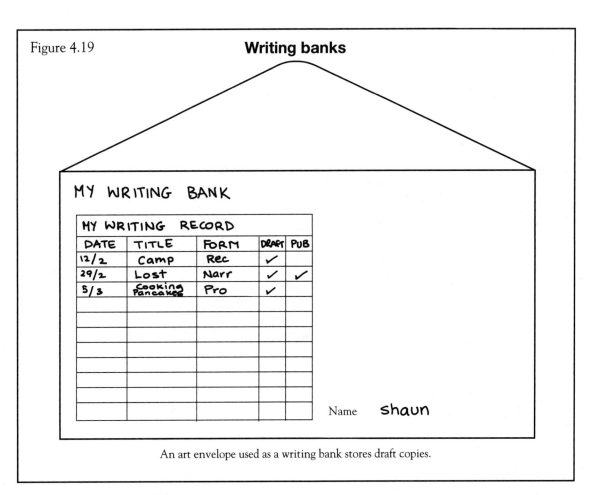

Figure 4.19   **Writing banks**

MY WRITING BANK

MY WRITING RECORD				
DATE	TITLE	FORM	DRAFT	PUB
12/2	Camp	Rec	✓	
29/2	Lost	Narr	✓	✓
5/3	Cooking Pancakes	Pro	✓	

Name   shaun

An art envelope used as a writing bank stores draft copies.

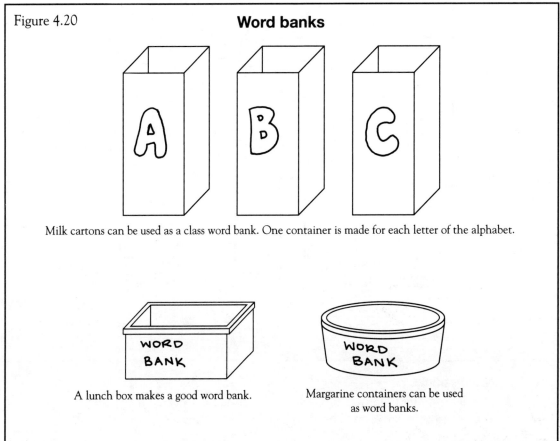

Figure 4.20   **Word banks**

Milk cartons can be used as a class word bank. One container is made for each letter of the alphabet.

WORD BANK

A lunch box makes a good word bank.

WORD BANK

Margarine containers can be used as word banks.

The folder is a valuable record of progress and development of the child's written language and is valuable for assessment and evaluation purposes.

Included on the front of this folder is a record sheet entitled 'What I have written about'. It is completed by the child each time work is placed into the folder and is used to keep a check on the amount of writing the child has completed, the style of writing attempted and whether they are drafts or published works.

A word bank

This is a well-sealed container in which can be stored those words taken from the child's writing that need to be learnt (see Figure 4.20).

A word wallet

This is an envelope used to store those words selected from the word bank to be learnt at a particular time. This word wallet is small enough to be kept in the word bank (see Figure 4.21).

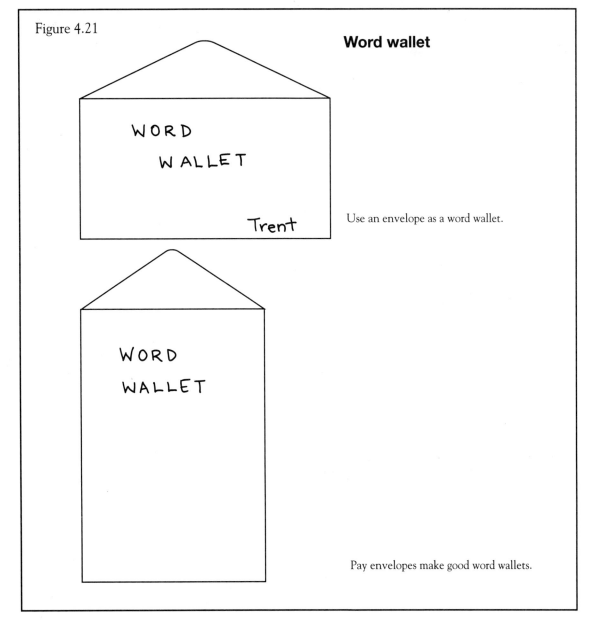

Figure 4.21

Word wallet

WORD WALLET

Trent

Use an envelope as a word wallet.

WORD WALLET

Pay envelopes make good word wallets.

Select words from the word bank to put into the word wallet.

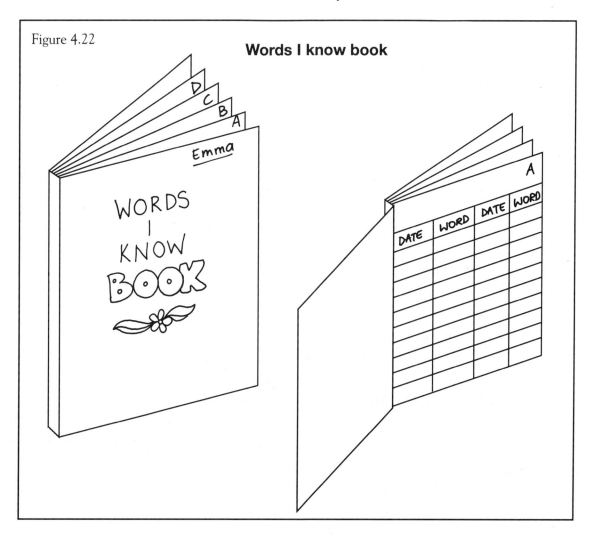

Figure 4.22

Words I know book

'Words I know' book

This book is used by the children to record, in alphabetical order (and with the relevant date), those words they can spell correctly. An indexed exercise book with each page ruled into columns is suitable (see Figure 4.22).

Have-a-go cards or sheets

The children need a personal have-a-go card on which they record their attempts at the correct spelling of words.

Language book

This general activity book is used for recording specific focus information or tasks. It may be used to record directed writing tasks, contract or elective activities.

The role of the teacher

The teacher needs to assume the following responsibilities as listed below.

- Provide a classroom environment conducive to developing competent writers.
- Provide models of the writing process. This involves both explicit modelling through demonstrations of writing activities and implicit modelling through the reading of texts and related discussion.
- Generate curiosity and interest in our language.
- Foster children's personal concern for their own writing ability and teach them the need for conventional spelling and grammar in given contexts.
- Establish a classroom climate that encourages children to 'have-a-go' and take risks in order to develop as competent language users.
- Plan writing opportunities and intervene when opportunities arise to discuss appropriate spelling or grammar usage.
- Understand how children develop as language users and be able to use this knowledge to provide appropriate activities.
- Emphasise the positive aspects of children's attempts at spelling and grammar and focus on what is correct in the children's attempts.
- Create a co-operative learning atmosphere in which children are encouraged to interact with their peers in order to seek help or advice with their written language problems.
- Become an efficient, astute 'kid watcher' in order to provide appropriate interventions in children's learning as well as observing and recording children's writing progress.
- Keep cumulative, dated samples of children's written work and ensure a variety of genres is collected to show children's writing development within different contexts.
- Plan and use the content or subject areas as a source of the language activities.
- Empower children to assume joint responsibility for their progress.
- Allow for large time blocks rather than smaller separate units of time.
- Understand the role of 'temporary' or 'invented' spelling in children's writing and encourage children to use these 'language markers' in lieu of 'safe', less challenging or appropriate words.

- Understand that the use of 'incorrect' grammar in children's oral and written language is temporary and with encouragement, correct modelling and time the children will use conventional grammar.
- Teach the strategies that enable children to learn how to spell words. This can be done during individual conferences, 'focus activities' or group conferences.

PROGRAM PLANNING

Introduction

This section outlines the principles on which I have based my program, the elements that need to be included in the program and aspects to consider when planning a program for each stage of spelling development.

Principles underlying the program
General

Children need to:

- write often to develop and practise their growing knowledge about written language
- read often to develop their vocabulary and understanding of how words are put together to convey meaning
- see the teacher model writing to realise how all writers work. They need to see how writers write—how they deal with spelling, punctuation and grammar problems
- read and write using a variety of styles in order to understand the ways language can be used
- take responsibility for their learning and participate in self-correction
- proofread their own writing or others' writing for spelling, punctuation and grammatical errors

Children make the links between reading and writing.

- have an active part in evaluating their progress towards writing competency
- feel owners of classroom resources and develop confidence in using these
- use temporary or invented grammar and spelling as a step towards conventional writing.

Spelling

Children need to:

- have the opportunity to hear, say, see and write words as often as possible
- use words in a variety of contexts
- understand the importance of the link between handwriting and spelling and write clearly and fluently
- select from their own writing the words they wish to learn to spell
- know the procedures for learning to spell
- be trained to take note of the various strategies they use to spell
- be trained to notice words, to be curious about words and be enthusiastic users of words. They need to experiment and have fun with words and become 'word watchers'
- feel owners of classroom resources and develop confidence to add to, compile or make word lists, activities, or games
- be trained to use the look–say–look again–cover–write–check, method when learning to spell a particular word. Figure 5.1 is an adaptation of Cripps C and Peters M (1988) routine for learning the spelling of a new word.

Figure 5.1

Look	The child looks carefully at the word. This first glance at the word is to identify the word, that is, basic word recognition. This first look is to take in fleeting information on the word and gain an overall view of the word.
Say	The child says the word, engaging the auditory skills, so the pronunciation can be checked. The following instructions can be used to help children: <ul><li>say the word slowly</li><li>break it into chunks</li><li>what sounds can you hear?</li></ul>
Look again	While looking at the word, the child can say it slowly. This second look can be used to look into the word and note the details. The following instructions can be used to help children: <ul><li>Can the word be broken into chunks?</li><li>What is the tricky part?</li><li>Underline this part.</li><li>What is the shape of the word?</li><li>Try to photograph the word onto your eyelids.</li><li>What can you do to help you remember how to spell the word?</li></ul>
Cover	The child covers the word.
Write	The child attempts to write the whole word from memory.
Check	The word is uncovered and if it is not spelt correctly the child underlines the incorrect part and takes note of the correct parts of the attempt and then repeats the above procedure.

The program needs:

- to include discussion of meaning and origins of words
- an emphasis on the uses of words in our language
- an emphasis on noting the structures and patterns and details in words
- to provide practice in using visual memory for words.

Grammar

Children need to:

- read and write different writing forms for a variety of audiences and purposes
- read and discuss how these texts have been structured
- write texts and be able to identify how they can be improved
- identify the function of some parts of speech in texts.

Reading and discussing texts helps children understand the patterns and use of our language.

The program needs:

- to include discussion and analysis of texts
- to provide modelling of correct grammatical forms
- an emphasis on the parts of speech only in the writing context
- an emphasis on the rhythms and patterns and moods of language that can be created through careful selection and organisation of words.

Components of the program

Talk about words

Talk about their meanings, their sounds, their origins and how they can be used.

Talk about texts

Talk about how the words are put together to convey meaning and how the sentences are organised to impart more information.

Play with words

Add letters to form new words, delete letters to create another word, use the words in sentences, make up word puzzles, or make up original words.

Play with texts

Be innovative with texts, rearrange the sentences, add or substitute words.

Look into words

Note their letter patterns, look for words within words, note the shape of the words, note the letter sequences, find the difficult or tricky parts of words.

Look into texts

Note how the information is grouped, the writing form used, the purpose of the text.

Visualise words

Encourage children to 'photograph' words so that they can form a visual memory of the complete words.

Visualise texts

Encourage children to form a mental picture of the image created by the text.

Write words

Encourage children to write words from memory, not to copy letter by letter. Play games that need written responses, create lists, write as often as possible.

Write texts

Encourage children to be innovative with text patterns, to create texts using the same grammatical features and to experiment with other forms of writing.

Listen to words

Listen to the sounds in words, listen for the syllables or suggest rhyming words.

Listen to texts

Listen to the patterns of the language, listen to the use of particular parts of speech and listen to the way the text is organised.

Children construct a chart using words with a given letter pattern.

Collect words

Set up tasks that require children to look for and collect words with a particular focus. Collect homophones, anagrams, portmanteau words, onomatopoeic words, acronyms, specific visual or sound patterns, plurals.

Collect texts

Display texts that demonstrate specific language structures. Collect examples of well-written texts. Collect poems, sayings, metaphors, reports, procedural texts, descriptive texts or scripts.

Group words

Classify words according to visual patterns, sound patterns, meanings, root words, number of syllables or origins.

Group texts

Classify texts according to given criteria, for example, amusing texts, sad texts, informative texts, factual or fictional texts.

Take risks with words

Encourage children to attempt the spelling of unknown words, to use an extensive vocabulary and be adventurous with words.

Take risks with text

Encourage children to be adventurous and experiment with our language. Encourage them to write in different forms for different purposes and audiences. Help them use learnt conventions.

Make up gimmicks for words

Encourage children to create memory aids that will help them spell irregular or difficult words.

Make up gimmicks for texts

Create sentences that use alliteration, use many adjectives or include adverbs. Help children to understand the function of different parts of speech.

Think about words

Suggest alternative words, build up an extensive oral vocabulary, think about the meanings of words.

Think about texts

Think of how to express the same meaning in a variety of ways. Think what a given text would be like if parts were substituted, for example, all the adjectives were substituted with antonyms.

Elements to be included in program planning

Daily

- build on children's written language competencies
- plan activities to centre on a spelling and/or grammar focus
- provide time for children to tend to their own spelling and/or grammar needs

- provide opportunities to write every day
- program for the implicit and explicit modelling of correctly written forms
- demonstrate the many uses of written language
- immerse children in print, in many different forms, for different purposes and audiences
- conduct incidental spelling and grammar demonstrations as they arise
- create an awareness of words
- conduct individual or group conferences
- let spelling and grammar be seen as part of all written activities
- look for common spelling or grammar needs that can become the basis for focus studies
- provide opportunities to read and discuss a variety of texts.

Weekly

- look at the topic for the week and draw language activities from this
- establish a spelling and/or grammar focus or focuses for either the class, group or individual
- provide time for children to read, write and discuss texts
- allow children to select their own words to learn during the week
- provide time for partner testing of these words at the end of the week
- link reading and writing activities across the curriculum
- look for opportunities or resources that will extend children's spelling and/or grammar knowledge
- build up a curiosity in words and encourage children to collect words of interest
- encourage 'looking for' and 'looking into' words
- enter correctly spelt words into a Words I know book.

Monthly

- allow time for children to collect from Words I know books all the words they have learnt during the month. These are written by the children and filed away in their language profiles
- provide revision activities based on the month's spelling and/or grammar focuses
- encourage student self-evaluation and reflection on their written language; they can use checklists, learning logs or self-evaluation sheets
- provide time for children to add their contributions to class books or charts
- conduct teacher evaluation of common errors, needs and strengths, as revealed through the study of children's written language
- celebrate individual and group achievements in writing
- record, through anecdotal records, the achievements and needs of children.

Model of language session

The following language session is based on a two-hour period of time.

USSR—15–20 minutes

This period involves children in browsing, selecting and reading books of their own choice.

Focus session—15–20 minutes

This period usually involves the whole class or small groups and involves the demonstration, modelling or explanation of some aspect of written language. It may be a writing form or a spelling, grammar or punctuation focus. The focus is usually drawn from a text used in the unit of work.

Exploration—15–20 minutes

This activity may be related to the focus study and may involve group or individual participation. Conferences or clinics may be held during this time.

Share time—5 minutes

This may involve the sharing of individual group or class activities based on the focus or the exploration.

Focus session—15 minutes

This session may include another demonstration of some aspect of language as mentioned earlier, or it may be a serial story, poetry or a specific reading–writing model. It may also include instructions or explanations of the work to follow.

Individual work—35 minutes

Children work on their own language needs. Some will attend to directed or compulsory activities while others will proceed with personal work.

Share time—5 minutes

This may involve the sharing of individual or group activities that have been attempted.

A one-hour session

If only one hour blocks of time are available the following format could be adapted to individual teacher's programming needs. This format is also suitable for use with younger children.

Focus—15 minutes

This session may involve serial story reading, shared books, jointly constructed texts, modelled reading–writing, singing, oral work or poetry.

USSR—10 minutes

This may involve children browsing, selecting and reading books of their own choice.

Reading–writing focus—10 minutes

This involves a demonstration of some aspect of reading or writing. It may be based on a particular writing form. For writing, it may be based on a spelling, punctuation or grammar focus. For reading, it may be based on the structure, content or response to a text.

Activity time—20 minutes

This involves participation in whole class, small group or individual activities based on the reading–writing focus.

Share time—5 minutes

This may involve the sharing of individual or group activities that have been attempted.

Example of a week's focus and individual strands

These sessions are approximately 15–20 minutes in duration and are part of the language periods. They can be planned or incidental sessions and involve implicit or explicit demonstrations of written language.

Session one
- introduction to the focus through a written model
- this focus may be presented to a whole class or groups
- discussion about the focus
- set up tasks related to the focus which are to be continued during the week, for example, research tasks or set up charts
- children then select from their word banks the words they wish to learn during the week
- these words are placed into the word wallets
- progression into session.

Sessions two, three and four
- alternative applications of focus study using a variety of models, texts, activities or the introduction to a new focus study
- individuals work on their own spelling words
- individuals select from a class chart particular activities to do with their own words
- the activities children use for their own words are general enough to apply to individual words
- progression into session.

Session five
- a teacher-devised assessment strategy based on a week's focus/focuses may be conducted, for example, spelling or grammar cloze, directed writing activity or proofreading activity
- partner testing or individual words from word wallets
- correct words are entered into Words I know books with appropriate date
- errors are placed back into word banks for further learning
- progression into session.

A weekly program

This may consist of a list of daily or weekly objectives or focuses and the activities planned to achieve these. The language activities and specifically the focus studies, would be planned after the content areas of the curriculum or the topic to be covered have been decided.

Program planning for developmental stages

The objectives of the programs for all stages should be to:

- encourage children to read a wide range of reading materials
- provide opportunities for personal writing every day

Children working on their writing. They are all at different stages.

- include modelled writing to demonstrate writing for different purposes and audiences
- provide opportunities for writing across the curriculum
- provide opportunities for children to experiment with writing and to learn about spelling as they write
- compile word lists that are grouped so children can see either the visual patterns or the meaning relationships in words
- provide opportunities for children to classify words
- develop self-correction strategies
- enable children to form their own generalisations about spelling
- develop a multisensory approach to the learning of spelling.

Precommunicative stage

Objectives of the program should be to include the above aspects plus:

- develop children's interest in print
- demonstrate that print conveys meaning and this meaning is unchanged with each reading
- introduce the terms, letters, words, sentences, sounds and help children recognise each of these in context; this can be done through print walks
- teach the letter names
- enable children to distinguish sounds at the beginning or end of words; this can be done through auditory activities
- enable children to listen for, recognise or suggest rhyming words
- encourage the correct pronunciation of words
- encourage children to write.

Semiphonetic stage

The objectives of the program should be to include the above aspects plus:

- develop a willingness to write
- develop children's knowledge of alphabetical order
- develop the ability to divide words into sound parts
- encourage the use of invented spelling
- compile personal word banks of known words
- enable children to listen for sounds in words
- enable children to distinguish sounds in different positions in words
- enable children to recognise upper- and lower case letters
- enable children to write words by representing sounds in the order in which they hear them
- set up word lists to which children can refer when writing
- compile lists of high frequency words.

Phonetic stage

The objectives of the program should be to include the above aspects plus:

- develop and use alphabetical lists to record words as they arise in activities
- develop the understanding that a sound can be represented in several different ways
- develop the understanding that a letter or letters can represent more than one sound in particular words
- develop an emphasis on the visual features of words
- enable children to represent sounds with a letter or letters
- explore the sound–symbol relationships
- develop children's understanding that letters have names and not sounds and that letters represent sounds only when in a word
- enable children to write capital and lower-case letters
- enable children to recognise letters by shape and letter name
- provide opportunities to group words
- encourage children to proofread their own known words
- introduce the use of have-a-go cards.

Transitional stage

The objectives of the program should be to include the above aspects plus:

- extend children's vocabulary through a variety of purposeful oral activities
- encourage children to attempt alternative spellings until correct spelling is recognised
- develop children's ability to identify base words and develop word building skills
- create opportunities to generalise about words
- provide opportunities for children to classify words according to visual patterns
- develop children's resource skills
- extend children's knowledge of plural formations
- encourage syllabification
- extend the use of personal word banks
- emphasise the visual patterns in words

- encourage the use of mnemonics to remember difficult words
- explore the sound–symbol relationships
- develop a range of strategies for remembering new words
- develop an awareness of words that are spelt the same, but may be pronounced differently according to their use in texts
- emphasise the importance of correct spelling for an audience
- extend children's knowledge of homophones
- teach effective proofreading
- develop an awareness of correct spelling in the environment
- focus on the meaning relationships between words, for example, sign, signature, signal or design.

Correct spelling stage

The objectives of the program should be to include the above aspects plus:

- develop children's responsibility for their own spelling corrections
- emphasise the role of the draft when writing
- enable children to use a variety of strategies to spell words
- focus on the meaning of words to help with the spelling of words
- further develop the use of references—
  ability to select appropriate definitions
  ability to write concise definitions
  ability to use a range of dictionaries
  ability to use a thesaurus for the selection of synonyms and antonyms
  ability to effectively use an encyclopaedia to acquire information
- enable children to select the most appropriate strategy when spelling an unfamiliar word
- further develop proofreading skills
- focus on the derivation of words
- explore the origins of words
- explore eponyms
- recognise and use comparative and superlative adjectives
- facilitate extensive vocabulary development
- develop children's ability to select more appropriate words to use.

ACTIVITIES

Introduction

This section includes some activities that could help extend children's knowledge about spelling and grammar. They have been grouped according to specific skills and strategies that may need to be developed. Teachers may adapt these activities to meet individual, group or class needs as required.

Proofreading

The best activity to develop children's writing competencies and understandings is that of proofreading and correcting their own writing. Through this children are trained to identify, correct and learn from their own errors. The mistakes revealed in proofreading can be used as part of the teaching–learning process.

Children need to be taught what proofreading means and what it entails. So often children say they have proofread their work, but really do not know how to do it effectively. The teacher needs to model the proofreading process. This can be done in several ways during:

- modelled writing in which the activity is to demonstrate proofreading skills
- focus activities in which a text specifically constructed by the teacher is used to help with the modelling of the process
- joint proofreading of a constructed text
- partner activities in which children help each other proofread their work

- whole class activities in which a class member's piece of writing is proofread (with the child's permission, of course).

Children need to be aware that proofreading involves the following:

- checking to see if the text makes sense
- ensuring that the information is arranged logically
- checking that spelling, grammar and punctuation are correct
- eliminating overused words
- substituting better words
- varying sentence beginnings
- expanding sentences.

The teacher needs to explain that proofreading is different to reading. In reading, the details of each word are not looked at closely. In proofreading each word has to be looked into carefully and each letter noted. Explain how publishers employ people who proofread for spelling and how they 'word call' without reading for meaning.

It may help the children to place a ruler under each line of their writing and use a pencil to point to each word as they say it. This procedure helps to identify word omissions or additions as well as helping to focus children's attention on individual words.

Children need to circle the words of which they are not sure. This procedure can even be used with very young children. They can also underline the parts of sentences to query the grammatical correctness.

With older children some of the devices used by publishers when proofreading can be introduced and explained. It is best to leave some time between the writing and the proofreading stage so that errors are more readily identified.

Spelling activities

Activities should only be chosen if they can be seen to be of value in developing a particular strategy or understanding. Ideally the activities should involve a written task, as spelling is only relevant in the written context. Well-chosen activities can help children discover information and form their own generalisations about our spelling system. The peer coaching that often takes place during such activities is valuable in the child's learning process.

During spelling activities teachers are able to observe behaviours, analyse children's needs and intervene immediately to help the learner develop the appropriate spelling strategies involved in the activity. See the reference section at the back of the book for further comprehensive sources of activities.

Activities with topic words

Topic words are a very useful resource as children are writing within the subject. Words related to the topic being studied can be collected at the beginning and during the study of the topic. They can be collected as a brainstorm activity, as part of a text search or as the topic is investigated. Whole class, small groups or individuals can compile a topic list.

As the words are collected they need to be displayed so that they can be referred to as required. It is not advisable to ask children to learn to spell these words just because the common thread is the topic. Words need to be selected from the topic chart according to a common spelling strategy. For example:

- same visual pattern
- same sound or meaning connection.

Make sure children understand the reason for the grouping of the words that are to be studied.

The words on the topic chart can also provide the introduction to, discussion of and further exploration of words with the same characteristic. For example:

- the topic word chart may include the words 'thought' and 'enough'
- the pattern 'ough' is discussed and a further list is formed of any words that include this pattern, such as, bough, cough, and through.

From the topic words chart further lists can be made and focus studies can be developed.

When selecting words to be studied, teach the word groups so that children see the relationships between words. For example:

- catch, catching, caught
- get, getting, got
- do, doing, does
- done, doesn't, undo.

Try to use as big a visual pattern as possible when grouping words. This pattern selection aids children's visual memory development. For example:

- 'ough' is a better pattern than the 'ou' pattern
- 'ake' is a better pattern than the 'a–e' pattern.

The topic list words can be used for word sort activities which enable children to form their own generalisations about spelling. Children are required to sort the words in one of the following methods:

- **closed word sorts** in which words are classified by teacher directed criteria
- **open word sorts** in which children may group the words according to their own criteria.

The topic words should be used as a valuable spelling resource and as a basis of word study activities. They need to be used as the means of helping children learn about spelling.

Activities with personal words

Children need to learn their own personal spelling and the best learning activity is a written one. The following activities are general enough, that all children can apply them to their own words. Children would not be expected to do each activity. The teacher may select a couple to be done each day. For example, for each of your words:

- write the word and the word shape
- write the base word

- word build
- mark in the syllables
- write another word which has the same letter pattern
- write another word that has one of the same sounds in it
- write a rhyming word–synonym–antonym
- write the dictionary meaning
- use a thesaurus to write words of similar meaning
- write a sentence which includes the word
- write all the smaller words you can find in it
- underline the tricky part.

Use all of the words and:

- group them according to the number of syllables
- group them according to their letter patterns
- group them according to their sounds
- group them according to similar meanings
- arrange them in alphabetical order
- group them according to your own criteria.

When children are selecting their personal words to learn, it is advisable that all related words are learnt at the same time. This enables children to make connections between words that will aid their spelling of them. For example:

- wrap, wrapped, wrapping, unwrap
- receive, receiving, receptionist, reception.

Teach children strategies to help them remember how to spell difficult words. For example:

- help children identify the difficult part in words—
  what, believe, half
- make up gimmicks to help children remember how to spell particular words—
  you must have a **pie** before you have a **pie**ce
- help children see the patterns in different sounding words—
  thought, **though**, **bough**, **enough**
- use a multisensory approach to help children see what a word looks like, hear the sounds in the word and feel how the word is written.

General activities

These activities can be adapted to help develop any of the strategies.

Word sorts

This activity enables children to discover similarities and differences between words and can be designed to develop visual, phonetic or morphemic knowledge. All that is required is a list of words which children are required to classify according to teacher directed categories or to student determined categories. For example:

- group all the double letter words
- group words with two vowels
- group words with the same sound.

Text searches

Children are asked to scan given texts and locate and write (within a given time limit) those words that fit the criteria stated by the teacher. The winner is the team or individual with the most words correctly written. For example,

children may be asked to find words that:

- begin with **b**
- are plurals
- end in **ing**
- have double letters.

Five tasks

The teacher has a series of spelling tasks written on cards which are stored in a tin. These are drawn out one by one by the teacher and read quickly to the children. If children can think of a word for each task as it is read out they write it down. If not, they wait for the next task to be read out. As children complete five tasks they call out and these are corrected. The winner is the child with five correctly spelt words that match five of the tasks. For example:

Write a word that has a prefix.	Write a compound word.	Write a word that comes from the Greek root 'kilo'.
Write a word that has the letters **ear** in it.	Write a word that has the **o** sound in it.	Write a word that rhymes with **play**.

For younger children this activity may entail the following:

Write the letter at the beginning, middle or end of **sat**.	Write a word that begins with **b**.	Write the word from this list that rhymes with **Jack**: lick, sack, suck.

Noughts and crosses

This can be played in teams or with partners. Children are asked to spell specific words. If the word is written correctly a mark can be placed on the noughts and crosses grid. If the word is written incorrectly the player is unable to write on the grid.

Written conversation

This activity involves all communication to be written. It can be a teacher, group–individual or a partner activity. It is a valuable activity to encourage reluctant writers. It is a useful assessment strategy for the teacher.

Word sausages

This game is played in pairs or in teams. The teacher sets a particular criteria for the words to be used. For example:

- words with the same sound
- words with the same letter pattern
- words with the same number of syllables
- theme or topic words
- synonyms, eg synonyms for 'little'
- words that are alternatives, eg better words than 'said'.

Children are required to take turns writing words and the team–individual that misspells a word, or cannot write any more words, loses. For example:

- an **a** sound word sausage—day mate rain play great eight.

Word bank bingo

Children may use words from their word banks for this activity. They select 10 words from their word banks and place them face up on the table. When the teacher gives out a specific clue those children who have a word to fit the given criteria turn the word face down. For example:

- turn over any word you have that has a prefix
- turn over any word you have that has a double letter
- turn over any word you have that has the letters **ai**.

When they have turned over three (or an agreed number of words) they call out 'bingo'.

Word webs

Children are required to write as many words as they can that can be associated with a given topic. These words can then be grouped under further headings.

This can also be played where a particular word plus specific headings is given and children must complete as much of this table within a given time limit.

Yes–no game

This is played in teams and is a very good activity to encourage children to think about words and to look carefully at them.

Two columns headed 'yes' and 'no' are drawn up. In the 'yes' column the first team writes three words that share similar criteria. In the 'no' column one word that doesn't share this criteria is written.

The second team suggests words for the 'yes' column. If these words fit the criteria they are written in the column and if not they are written in the 'no' column. After four extra words have been added to the chart the second team may actually state why they think the words are in the 'yes' column. If the team guesses the criteria a point is awarded and a new game commences. The team with the most points wins.

Steps and stairs

Children can use all the words from their word banks for this activity. They are required to place their word strips so that the last letter of the previous word determines the first letter of the next word to be placed down. The child with the most steps in a given time span is the winner. For example:

• out of all the words in a child's word bank the following five steps and stairs could be made.

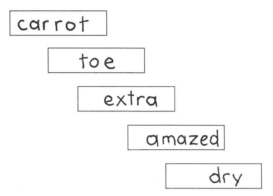

Alternatively it can be played in pairs in which children take turns writing any words that begin with the last letter of the word written by the other child. The winner is the child who doesn't make a spelling mistake.

The activity can be adapted so that particular letter patterns or sound patterns must be used.

Take two

This game is played with letter tiles such as those used in 'Scrabble'. All the tiles are placed face down and the players each select seven tiles which they place face down in front of them. At the starting signal they can turn over the tiles and build words. When a player uses all of the seven tiles 'take two' is called out and all players must take a further two tiles from the face down tiles pool. This procedure is repeated until all tiles from the pool are used and one player has been able to construct words using all of the personal tiles.

At the end of the game one point is scored for each letter used and the winner is the player with the highest score.

Word cross

This game is played with letter tiles. All the tiles are placed face down and the players each select 15 tiles which they place face down in front of them. At the starting signal they must make as many interlocking words as possible within a three-minute time limit.

At the end of the game one point is scored for each letter used and two points for those letters used to connect two words. The winner is the player with the highest score.

Five questions

This activity is designed to encourage children to develop general terms about our language, as well as specific information about individual words. One player selects a word from a list that is in view of all the players. The remaining players are able to ask five questions (or a nominated number) about the word, which can only be answered with 'yes' or 'no'. If the word is guessed before the five questions are completed, the team gains a point. If the word is incorrectly guessed at any time during the question time the team forfeits the rest of their turn. For example:

- does the word have double letters?
- does it have two syllables?
- are their two vowels in it?

Time limit activities

Children are set a task that has to be completed within a given time limit. For example:

- write all the words you can think of that have **ear** in them
- list all words in which you can hear the **a** sound.

Crosswords

Crosswords that include either phonetic, visual or meaning clues can be constructed by the teacher.

Activities for visual strategy

These activities, while designed to help develop children's visual strategies, can be adapted for other strategies.

Spelling cloze

This activity can be conducted in a small group or individual situation. Children are given a text in which specific letter information has been omitted from some of the words. For example:

- omit initial letter/s
- omit middle letter/s
- omit final letter/s
- give initial letters only
- provide word shape
- provide letter blanks.

Finding words within words

Children are required to list all the words they can find within a larger word. For example:

- **stretcher**—her, etch, stretch.

Matching word shapes to words

A series of words is provided and the appropriate word shapes need to be matched together. For example:

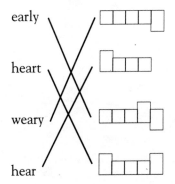

Word fits

A shape is drawn and children have to see how many words they can write that fit into the shape. For example:

- write words that have the following pattern.

Alternatively shapes of parts of words can be drawn and children must write as many words as possible that include the pattern. For example:

- write words that end with this pattern

- write words that begin with this pattern

- write words that begin with this pattern.

Word searches using grids

Children are required to locate all the words hidden among random letters on a grid. These words may:

- be theme or topic words
- have similar visual patterns
- have the same sound pattern.

Word links

This is similar to word search but the words are hidden in a string of letters instead of a grid. Children circle the words as they are found. When they have located all the words they must work out the common characteristic in all of the words. For example:

Kim's game

A series of words is written on individual cards (the number of words used is dependent on children's stage of development). Children look at each of the words until they are instructed to look away while one of the words is removed. They have to write correctly the word that was removed. The spelling can be checked by replacing the card.

Hangman

A player thinks of a word and writes a dash for each of the letters in the word. The second player suggests one letter at a time that may be in the word. If correct, the letter is written on the corresponding dash. If incorrect, part of the gallows is drawn. The second player wins if the word is guessed before the gallows is completed.

An adaptation of the above is for the first player to write the first letter only of the word and the remaining letters have to be guessed.

Find the word

Provide words in which children must find the smaller word for a given clue or clues. For example:

- find the parts of your body in these words—
  hearth, slipper, ship, early, farmer
- find an insect in the word elephant.

Hide the word–letter patterns

Provide children with a specific letter pattern and ask them to write the best words they can think of to 'hide' the letters. For example:

- hide **ear** in words
- hide **cei** in words.

Fill words

A series of letters and blanks which could be a word are provided by the teacher. Children create as many words as they can by providing letters for the blanks. The team or child with the most correct words is the winner. For example:

- how many words can you make by filling the blanks?

  _ R _ C _

What's the message?

A familiar saying is written with the vowels missing. Children have to decode it by providing the vowels. For example:

- ths ctvty s gd fr dvlpng wrnss f vwls.

Word weaving

A number of words are hidden in a grid. Children may start with any letter and move in any direction, one square at a time, to form a word. Each letter can only be used once for each word. The winner is the child with the most letters linked up at the end of the game. For example:

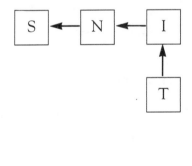

What won't be next?

This activity, which is played in teams, is designed to develop children's knowledge of the probability of letter sequences. Dictionaries will need to be available to check the responses.

The teacher writes a letter on the chalkboard and poses the following type of question:

What letter would not be next to this letter at the beginning of a word? For example:

- S _
- the first team suggests a letter that would not follow the given letter
- it is the task of the second team to check the correctness of the response by using the dictionary if necessary
- if the response is correct the first team gains a point, but if a word beginning with the given letter and the suggested letter is found the second team gains the point.

What's the word?

One child starts writing a word, letter by letter. The other child tries to guess the word. If the guess is correct the second child must finish writing the word. For example:

- first child writes the letter **c**
- second child guesses 'children'
- first child writes the letters **cu**
- second child guesses 'cut'
- first child writes **cus**
- second child guesses 'custard'
- first child writes **cush**
- second child correctly guesses 'cushion' and finishes writing it.

Step words

A word is given and children are required to change this word to another given word within a given number of steps. Only one letter can be changed at a time and each step must be a word. For example:

- change the top word into the bottom word.

  N I C E

  _ _ _ _

  _ _ _ _

  _ _ _ _

  T A L K

- change the top word into the bottom word.

  D O G

  _ _ _

  _ _ _

  C A T

Activities for phonetic strategy

These activities, while designed to help develop children's phonetic knowledge, can be adapted for other strategies.

Sound ball

The teacher suggests a word and throws the ball to a child, who must provide a word that rhymes with the word given by the teacher and then throw the ball to another child, who must suggest another word. The game continues until a word is repeated or no other words can be suggested.

Homophone concentration

See instructions in Activities for morphemic strategies.

Make new words

Using a familiar word ask children to change the first letter to create a new word. For example:

- big
  pig
  dig
  jig

This activity can be adapted to substitute letters in other positions in the word. For example:

- big
  beg
  bug
  bag
- big
  bin
  bit

Word stars

Children are required to make as many words as possible which include the vowel and any of the letters in the outer circle. For example:

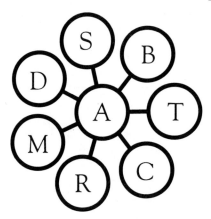

Locating rhyming words

Children may be asked to locate all the rhyming words in familiar poems and rhymes or texts. These words can then be grouped according to their letter patterns.

I spy

Children are asked to suggest an object, that they can see in the room, that begins with a certain letter. Use the letter name only. Discussion of the different sounds that letter represents can be conducted as individual words are suggested.

Alternatively, children may be asked to suggest an object, that they can see in the room, that begins with a certain sound. Discussion of the different letters that can represent the same sound can be conducted as individual words are suggested.

Syllable posts

Children are provided with several counters and a strip of cardboard divided into a series of sections. As the teacher says a word children are required to place a counter in each square according to the number of syllables in the word.

Sound bingo

Each player is provided with a card that has a series of words (or pictures) depicted on it. The teacher, or a child, reads out the information from sound task cards. If a player has a word that has this sound in it the word is covered with a counter. When a line of words or pictures is covered (in any direction) the player calls out 'bingo' and becomes the winner of that game.

Tongue twisters

Children are required to say known tongue twisters as quickly as possible without making a mistake.

They can be encouraged to create their own tongue twisters either orally or in written form.

Sound rummy

Pairs of words that have the same sound pattern are written on cards. The letters that represent the particular sound are underlined. For example:

Five cards are dealt to each player and the rest are placed face down in a pile, except for the top card which is placed face up to create a new pile. The first player may take the face up card or the first card on top of the face down pile. When the player has picked up one card they must discard one card from their hand and place it on the face up pile. The object of the game is to collect pairs of cards with the same sound pattern. As the players collect pairs they place these in front of them. The winner is the player who has the most pairs of cards when any player has no more cards in the hand.

Activities for morphemic strategies

These activities, while designed to help develop children's morphemic knowledge, can be adapted for other strategies.

Word building activities

- Build words from a single morpheme:
  form—forms, formed, former, forming, reform, deformed, formation.
- Build words from a given derivative:
  aqua—aquatic, aquamarine, aquarium, aqueduct.

- Build words from a given word but to a prescribed number of letters.
  For example:

build	sign
build _	sign _
build _ _	sign _ _
build _ _ _	_ _ sign
_ _ build	sign _ _ _ _ _

Affix snap

Pairs of cards with the same affixes need to be made. For example:

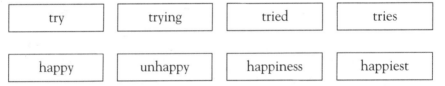

Each player is given a number of cards until all cards have been distributed. Each player in turn places one of their cards face up and if the added card matches the previous card the player that first calls 'snap' collects all the cards in the pile. The game is then repeated and the winner is the player with the most cards at the end of a given time.

Base word happy families

A series of four cards for each base word needs to be made and approximately 10 different sets are required. For example:

try	trying	tried	tries
happy	unhappy	happiness	happiest

The cards are dealt out to the children who arrange them into families. If they have any complete families they place these in front of them. The players then take turns to ask the other players if they have a card they require, for example, 'Darren, do you have a member of the **try** family?' If the child has the card then it is passed to the player who requested it and this player can continue asking other players until a request cannot be fulfilled. If a card cannot be provided the next player may take a turn at asking for cards. The winner is the player that makes the most families.

Homophone concentration

Pairs of cards with homophones need to be made. These cards are jumbled and placed face down in front of the players. Each player, in turn, turns over two cards. If they are a homophone match they are removed and piled in front of the player who then turns over another pair of cards. If a match is not made the cards are turned face down and the next player has a turn. The winner is the player with the most pairs of cards at the end of the game.

Plural race

In a given time children are required to write all the plurals that are formed a certain way. For example:

- write all the plurals you can think of that end in **ies**.

Match up

Match lists of words to make compound words.
For example:

foot   room
bed   table
time   ball

Select one word from each column to create a new larger word. For example:

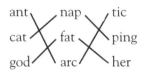

ant   nap   tic
cat   fat   ping
god   arc   her

Compound jigsaw

In this self-correcting activity parts of compound words are written on pieces of cardboard. Children are required to match up as many as possible in a given time. For example:

foot	ball
mush	room

Origin draw

A selection of basic Latin and Greek roots are written on cards which are then placed in a box. Teams take turns drawing a card from the box and saying the word and its meaning and then writing as many words that come from this root. A point is scored for each correctly spelt word. For example:

pes—Latin—foot	**finis**—Latin—end	**tele**—Greek—far	**autos**—Greek—self

Activities for resource skills

These activities are designed to develop children's knowledge of spelling resources.

Environmental print awareness activities

These activities help children to be aware of the print around the room and how these can be a spelling resource. For example:

Where would I find?~Divide the grade into two teams. Each team is given a word to find around the room. The team to locate the word first scores a point.

Print walks~At regular times conduct activities that involve children in reading the print around the room. For example:

- read the poems that are written on large sheets
- sing the song that is displayed
- revise the instructions that are written around the room
- jointly read the wall story.

How many words can you find?~Using only those words they can see around the room, children list the answers to the following type of tasks. For example:

- How many words can you find that have **air** in them?
- Write all the words you can see that have the **e** sound.
- Write as many words as you can that have three syllables.
- Find the word that means 'directions'.

Alphabet trails

The letters of the alphabet are arranged across a page. Children link up the letters in correct order. The letters can be arranged in shapes, such as animals, which children see when all the letters are joined up correctly.

Alphabetical order

These activities develop children's skills at alphabetical order. Children are required to sort the following into alphabetical order:

- random letters of the alphabet
- words with different first letters
- words with the same first letter and a different second letter
- words with same first and second letter.

Get into order~Children are divided into random groups of equal numbers. They are required to physically arrange themselves into order according to the alphabetical order of their names. The first group to do this is the winner. This can be made more difficult by increasing the size of the groups until all the class has to be arranged into alphabetical order.

Alphabetical order race

Children are organised into teams. A pile of cards (at least 24) which needs to be arranged in alphabetical order is placed face down a short distance from the teams. At the starting signal one player at a time from each team races up to the pile, grabs a card and places it face up in front of their team, then races back so the next player can repeat the process. The winning team is the team that has arranged 10 of the cards in correct alphabetical order.

Make a list

Children are given a word and are asked to list, in a given time span, all the words they can think of that are synonyms of the word. Use the thesaurus to check these lists.

Write the meaning

Children are given a word and asked to write its meaning as it would be in the dictionary. The dictionary is used to check their definitions.

Write the entry word

Children are given a word and are required to list the entry word it would be found under in the dictionary. They use the dictionary to check their answers. For example:

- write the entry word for **locally**.

Answer these

Children use the dictionary to find the answers to given questions.
For example:

* Would you eat a klieg?
* Do you have a hogget at home?
* Where would I find a patella?

Where will it be?

Suggest a word and children insert a bookmark into a closed dictionary where they think the word would be located. They check their accuracy with the dictionary.

What are these?

This activity is designed to encourage children to read dictionary meanings. Children are provided with a small word to which further letters can be added to create a word to fit the given meaning. For example:

* A can that is—
  made of wax   candle
  a disease   cancer
  a weapon.   cannon

* A car that is—
  a bottle   carafe
  towed by a vehicle   caravan
  a piece of clothing.   cardigan

Change the word

Provide a word which will require the changing of only one letter to form a new word to fit the given clue. Keep the first few letters the same to enable children to use the dictionary to find the new word. For example:

* change **load** into rich soil   loam
* change **heart** into the floor of a fireplace.   hearth

Activities for grammar

Like spelling, grammar is part of the writing process and is dealt with in this context. It should not be treated in isolated lessons but discussed as opportunities arise.

Because grammar has to do with the actual structure of our language to ensure meaning is expressed and understood, it is the actual process of writing that will develop grammatical knowledge. As with spelling, the best activity is the actual proofreading of children's own writing.

Modelling

Modelling, both planned and incidental, provides opportunities to develop children's knowledge of how our language is structured. It can be used to develop specific grammatical knowledge as well as all other aspects of language.

There are two forms of modelling that need to be incorporated into the classroom program.

Implicit modelling

Implicit modelling refers to the passive demonstrations of language through reading and listening. For example:

* Read to the children. Children are able to listen to the many forms and patterns of language.

- Read with the children. This can be during shared book time or other times as they arise. Children are able to see the correct written model and the teacher is able to draw children's attention to specific grammatical structures.
- Children read alone. Children are able to see the use of grammar to impart meaning.
- Present correct oral models. As the teacher interacts with children they are able to hear the correct use of our language.

Explicit modelling

Explicit modelling refers to the actual demonstration and explanation of how our written language is constructed.

- Write in front of the children. The teacher is able to discuss the grammatical decisions that need to be made as the text is written.
- Jointly construct texts with the children. As the text is being constructed grammatical decisions need to be made and these can be referred to using the correct terms, depending on the stage of development of children and the appropriateness to their needs.
- Discuss and analyse texts. The teacher can discuss the particular grammatical features of different writing forms.
- Participate in oral activities. Children are able to participate in activities designed to encourage them to speak clearly, correctly and logically.
- Clinics. As grammatical needs are revealed, small groups can be drawn together for demonstration and application sessions.
- Conference situations. During conferencing, specific grammatical knowledge and skills can be discussed as required.

Cloze activities

Children can complete cloze passages devised to require specific grammatical responses. For example:

- omit conjunctions, subjects, pronouns, verb tenses, adjectives.

Keep it going

The object of the game is to create a long and interesting sentence with a limited use of 'and'. This activity provides a starting point for discussion on the use of different parts of speech. It can be an oral or written activity.

The teacher–child starts off writing the first word of a sentence, the next child must add a word and then the next child and so on until a sentence is formed and cannot be extended. As children become familiar with this activity it will be necessary to add further limitations. For example:

- only three adjectives per noun
- only two adverbs per verb.

Touch and tell

An object is passed around the group and each member must suggest an adjective to describe it. For example:

- steel wool, corrugated cardboard, velvet, sandpaper, cottonwool or putty.

Pass the bag

An object is placed in a brown paper bag. The sealed bag is passed around the group and each member adds an adjective to describe what they feel in the bag.

Label the nouns

A picture, poster or photo is given to each group. Children have to write down all the things they see in the picture. These nouns can be grouped according to set or child decided criteria.

Sentence stretching

A brief sentence is written on a card which is then passed around the group. Each child must add one word to make the sentence more interesting. For example:

The lady crossed the road.

- The old lady crossed the road.
- The little old lady crossed the road.
- The little old lady slowly crossed the road.

Sentence building

Children are given a subject and within a given time they are required to create one intersting sentence about it. For example:

- the little puppy
- a tiny ant
- elephants.

Pass it on

The children sit in a circle and at the signal to start, write one sentence to begin a narrative. When the teacher says 'trade' the sentence is passed down two people. The new sentence is read and new sentences are added to form the middle section of the narrative. At the teacher's signal the sentences are passed down two more people and the procedure is repeated until the ending of the narrative is complete. The circle then forms into smaller groups to read the finished narrative and add suitable titles.

Verb draw

Selected pictures of animals, people, birds or objects that move are placed in a box. The children take turns to select a picture from the box. They write as many verbs for it within a given time. The winner is the child–group with the most verbs. This activity can be extended to include adverbs.

Silly sentences

Children suggest sentences which are formed according to a given pattern. These sentences are written on long strips of cardboard. Each strip is then cut into separate sections and each section is placed into a bag. Each player in turn takes a word from each bag and makes a stupid sentence (based on an activity suggested by Salmon 1987 p 26, see Figure 6.1).

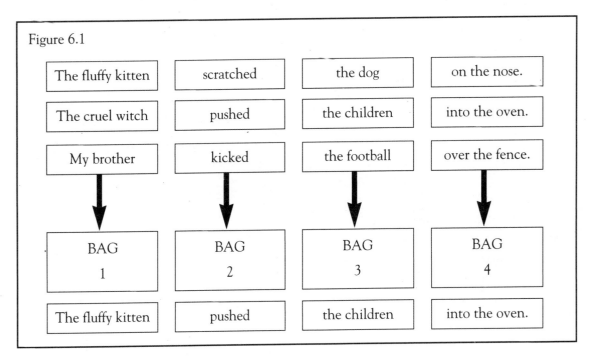

Figure 6.1

Daily dash

Children are asked to write non-stop for a given time in a particular writing form or on a particular subject.

Word dash

Within a given time children are asked to suggest all the verbs, nouns, adverbs or adjectives for a given subject. For example:

- Write all the actions you would see at the circus.
- Write all the ways you can speak.
- Write all the words you can think of to describe babies.

Toss and write

Children are asked to think about a given subject from six different aspects. They may need to list adjectives, verbs and adverbs associated with the subject or they may have to create a sentence, question or use alliteration to create a four word statement about the subject.

Children select a topic from the tin and then throw the cube. Whichever side of the cube faces up is the task they must attempt (see Figure 6.2).

Figure 6.2

ASSESSMENT AND EVALUATION

Introduction

In this section the ways in which spelling and grammar development can be assessed are outlined. How this information can be used for further program planning is discussed and the sources of information are described, as well as the strategies for recording this information.

Assessment and evaluation are an integral part of the learning process so it is necessary to decide how to assess children's progress and thus evaluate the program's effectiveness.

While spelling and grammar features are listed separately here, it is intended that they would become part of the knowledge the teacher brings to the observation of children, and their writing and assessment of their progress. It must be remembered that spelling knowledge will often be developed while discussing the function and arrangement of words in a text (grammar). Grammatical knowledge often will be developed when discussing the spelling of words in texts. Both aspects are intertwined.

Spelling—what to look for

Because spelling is a developmental processes there is a need to examine children's writing in the light of their stage of development, and when evaluating their progress look for development of the following spelling behaviours:

- sound–symbol knowledge
- visual memory development
- developing morphemic knowledge
- mastery of high frequency words
- location and use of spelling resources
- attempts to spell unknown words
- proofreading skills, for example, ability to locate, circle error and underline the part of which the child is unsure
- the use of inventive spelling in preference to 'safe' known words–spellings
- resource skills
- appropriate choice of strategies for writing unknown words
- attitudes towards spelling
- interest in and use of words.

Grammar—what to look for

Grammar is a developmental process, so the stage of development of the child needs to be taken into account when looking for the development of the following grammatical behaviours:

- ability to arrange words into meaningful units that make sense
- proofreading skills, for example, ability to locate error or underline the part of the text of which the child is unsure of the grammatical structure
- interest in the structure of our language
- use of developing grammatical knowledge to write more interesting texts
- developing knowledge and appropriate use of different parts of speech
- developing knowledge of the structure of different writing forms for different purposes and audiences.

Sources for assessment

The following sources can be used for children's spelling and grammar assessment:

- dated samples of children's writing
- observation of children during the writing process
- anecdotal records as a result of writing conferences and observations
- teacher devised activities, based on focus study work, for the purposes of providing information on the degree of application and understanding of the conventions discussed and to plan for further common spelling and grammar focuses, for example, cloze activities, directed writing, proofreading activities or dictionary work
- proofreading activities based on discovering the ways children go about locating and correcting spelling and/or grammar errors
- studying children's have-a-go cards
- examination of the individual child's Words I know book
- a spelling interview such as used in Bolton and Snowball (1985) could be used with those children about whom more information is needed in relation to their spelling attitudes.

Figure 7.1   **A work program**

TOPIC THE SEA   WEEK ENDING 2ND MAR

OBJECTIVES

To introduce reports – structure, function.
To introduce function of adjectives + adverbs in a text.
To emphasise many ways /a/ can be represented in words.
To emphasise the visual patterns of words.
To revise /ai/ for small group.

PLANNED FOCUSES

• Model report writing based on sea mammal.
• The way /a/ can be represented in words.
• Adding adverbs and adjectives to make report more informative.
• Beverley, Denise, Chris, Shaun + Ben to locate ai/ lettern pattern in words in shared book.
• Formation of adverbs. e.g 'ly' 'ily' + irregular.

ACTIVITIES

• Read series of reports. Discuss features.

• Construct report in front of class.

• Read and retell report.

• Set up week's task to find ways /a/ represented in words. Set up charts.

• Group /a/ words according to visual patterns.

• Groups begin cooperative construction of a report of sea animal.

• Cloze activity (omit adverbs).

• Children group own word bank words to set criteria (syllables, letter patterns).

Teacher records

Outline of yearly program

This would include the general objectives of the written language program, the anticipated focuses to be treated and an explanation of the way this program will be implemented.

Weekly program

This consists of a list of daily or weekly objectives or focuses and the activities planned to achieve these (see Figure 7.1).

Record of focuses covered

This consists of the focuses and includes the source of focus and the type of teaching situation used (see Figure 7.2).

Figure 7.2

FOCUSES COVERED

Focus	Form and date	Comments and source
Dictionary Skills	Whole Class 10/2	Tchr Direction.
Use of Have-A-Go	" " 12/2	" "
Basewords	" " 17/2	Sea Topic Words
Derivatives	Group 17/2	" " "
Verbs	Whole class 23/2	Locate in explanation about tides.
Verbs - Tenses	1/3 5/3 10/3	Shared Book "Down
Adverbs		Round About + Up Again."
Forming adverbs	Group 12/3	Jointly constructed text on sea mammals
Adjectives < $^{ier}_{iest}$	Whole class 16/3	Based on shared book "Longneck's Billabong."

Language anecdotal record folder

This comprises a page for each child on which the teacher writes relevant observations during or after group or individual conferences (see Figure 7.3).

Figure 7.3

WRITTEN LANGUAGE ANECDOTAL RECORDS

NAME Emma   GRADE 6

DATE	STAGE	TOPIC/FORM	COMMENTS
24/2	1st Draft	Zoo Excursion — Recount	Logical sequence of events. Varied sentence beginnings. Homophone confusion. e.g they're / there, where, wear
9/3	1st D	'Lost in Space' — Narrative	Wrote good lead sentence. Needs to vary use of 'went' + 'got'. Added adverbs during conferencing.
2/4	Pub	'Lost In Space'	Changed working title to "A Space Adventure". Partner proof reading found plural formation errors. Needs help with ways of publishing.
7/4	1 D.	Science Experiment	Spelling of 'apparatus' was 'aparartus' - phonetic Used dictionary to check for correct form.

Figure 7.4

SPELLING AWARENESS OBSERVATIONS

Exhibits writing-like behaviour.

Is curious about print.

Copies some letters.

Knows names of some letters.

Matches some sounds to letters.

Attempts to invent spellings.

Writes captions for own drawings.

Knows some words by sight.

Knows terms:

        sentences

        words

        letters

        sounds.

Willing to attempt to spell unknown words.

Represents most sounds in words with symbols.

Uses knowledge of common letter patterns in words.

Able to identify (circle) misspelt words.

Able to identify (underline) misspelt part of a word.

Uses visual strategies.

Uses morphemic knowledge.

Uses phonetic strategies.

Uses meanings of words to help with spellings.

Looks for words within words.

Developing proofreading skills:

        use of drafts

        location of errors

        correction of errors.

Uses a range of resources to locate spellings:

        class lists

        dictionary

        thesaurus

        personal dictionary

        other people.

Developing a range of strategies to remember how to spell new words.

        look–say–cover–write–check

        mnemonics

        visual

        morphemic

        graphophonic

        meaning.

Spelling awareness observations

These comprise a list of indicators of children's developing spelling and can be in the form of checklists or they can be used as guides for the writing of anecdotal records. The list is not prescriptive or exhaustive or necessarily in any order. The teacher could select a couple of criteria and observe children over a period of time. Observations can be entered in the anecdotal record sheet or a checklist could be made for the appropriate indicators (see Figure 7.4).

Student profiles

The teacher has a Manila folder for each child. It is used to hold samples of the child's work to enable the teacher to gain a complete picture of the child's written language development over a period of time.

Examples of children's work that could be included are:

• read and retell activities
• dated, completed have-a-go sheets
• monthly collections of words I know
• cloze sheets
• drafts collected periodically
• handwriting samples
• spelling self-evaluation sheets
• samples of proofreading activities
• samples of spelling and grammar focus activities.

Pupil self-evaluation

Apart from the resources mentioned earlier in this book the following records help children identify, monitor and assess their language development. Children need to reflect on what they know and how they know it. They need to verbalise their insights into language learning as this can make subsequent learning easier. They need opportunities to alter and refine their own understandings after sharing others' understandings.

Children also need to play an active part in the assessment of their spelling and grammar knowledge and this can be done by using some of the following ideas.

Things I know chart

This sheet can be attached to children's writing folders and as they feel they have achieved a milestone in their writing behaviours they record this, with the date, on the sheet. Because some children are reticent to acknowledge their achievements or are unable to view their work in terms of goals attained, some guidance will be necessary to help them (see Figure 7.5).

Learning log

This log is filled out regularly and is designed to help children reflect on their learning generally. In this log children are encouraged to record their feelings, attitudes, discoveries and queries about their knowledge and understandings of written language. The children need training to reflect,

Figure 7.5

Things I know

Name Alischa

DATE	
4/2	I know better words than went.
4/2	I know how to use a Thesaurus.
12/2	I know how to fill in my Words I Know Book.
14/2	I know how to write a recount.
20/2	I know how to add adjectives to sentences.
28/2	I know how to group words.
5/3	I know about suffixes and prefixes.
13/3	I know how to write interesting stories.
18/3	I know how to publish.
20/3	I know how to write a blurb.

Figure 7.6

12-4-91   Learning Log.

This term I have learnt how to write reports and narratives. I can write really interesting sentence beginnings. I use adjectives to make my writing more interesting. I learn my spelling best when I look at the word carefully and photograph the hard bits. I need to use the dictionary more to help me with my spelling.

because they will write recounts of their experiences or activities without thinking about how or why they have learnt (see Figure 7.6). They need to consider the following:

- what I have learnt
- how I learnt to...
- what helps–hinders my learning
- I learn best when...
- what I need to improve; how? why?
- what I am good at, enjoy, dislike; why?
- I'm not sure...

Self-evaluation checklist

Children should have the opportunity to judge their own progress towards becoming good spellers. A simple checklist that children could use periodically to record their attitudes and approaches towards spelling can be used (see Figure 7.7).

Writing conferences

These conferences give both the teacher and the individual child an opportunity to discuss, examine and decide on spelling and/or grammar

Figure 7.7

Name_____ Date_____

MY SPELLING CHECK

- I care about spelling.

  0 |___.___.___.___.___.___.___.___.___.___| 10

- I always check my spelling on my second draft.

  0 |___.___.___.___.___.___.___.___.___.___| 10

- I always carefully proofread before someone else reads my writing.

  0 |___.___.___.___.___.___.___.___.___.___| 10

- When I am learning a new word I look–say–look again–cover–write–and then check.

  0 |___.___.___.___.___.___.___.___.___.___| 10

		I know how to:
I say the word slowly.		
I divide it into parts.		
I underline the hard part.		
I check if the word looks right.		
I think of the base word.		
I think of different ways to write one sound.		

My teacher's comments:

achievements and areas for further development. They provide opportunities for shared language to be developed and allow the student to become aware of the various aspects of writing. These conferences also give the teacher insights into the further focus studies required and what clinic groups need to be formed.

Writing record sheet

This includes the date, title, form and stage of writing that the child has attempted. This form is filled out each time a piece of writing is no longer being used or worked on (see Figure 7.8).

Program evaluation

Having gained information it is important to use this to provide further learning experiences for the child.

A written language program can only be effectively evaluated by taking into consideration the following:

- the many forms of writing children have attempted
- the variety of purposes of writing that children have been exposed to and ultimately use
- the behaviours children exhibit towards developing themselves as competent language users
- the stages of development of each class member
- the attitudes and enthusiasm children exhibit towards the writing process and towards spelling and grammar awareness.

When do you evaluate?

It should:

- be a continuous and ongoing process
- take place whenever writing occurs
- occur during conferences and clinics
- occur when children are participating in activities.

Why do you evaluate?

To:

- find out what the child knows about our writing system
- plan for further teaching
- report to other teachers, parents and the child.

How do you evaluate?

Use:

- observation of children during the writing process
- teacher devised assessment strategies
- analysis of children's writing
- checklists
- error analysis strategies
- anecdotal records
- child self-evaluation strategies.

Figure 7.8

MY WRITING RECORD   Name_____

TITLE	FORM	DRAFT	PUBLISHED	DATE

MY WRITING RECORD   Name_____

TITLE	FORM	DRAFT	PUBLISHED	DATE

BIBLIOGRAPHY

The books marked with * are also a good source of spelling activities.

Bean, W and Bouffler, C *Spell by writing* PETA, 1987.

* *Spelling R-7 language arts* Education Department of South Australia, 1984.

* Bolton, F and Snowball, D *Springboards: ideas for spelling* Nelson, 1985.

Brown, H and Mathie, V *Inside whole language* PETA, 1990.

Cambourne, B *The whole story—natural learning and the acquisition of literacy in the classroom* Ashton Scholastic, 1988.

Collerson, John *Grammar part 1* PEN 77 PETA, 1990.

Collerson, John *Grammar part 2* PEN 78 PETA, 1990.

* Cripps, C and Peters, M *Catchwords: ideas for teaching spelling* Harcourt Brace Jovanovich, 1988.

Daly, E (ed) *Monitoring children's language development* ARA Carlton, 1989.

Emmitt, M and Pollock, J *Language and learning* Oxford University Press, 1991.

Forester, A, cited by Rivalland, J 'Teaching spelling: helping the developing speller' in *Australian journal of reading* vol 8, no 1, 1985.

* Gates, Heather 'Spelling games' in *Chalkface* Ministry of Education, Victoria, 1981.

Gentry, R 'An analysis of developmental spelling' in *GNYS AT WRK, The reading teacher*, vol 36 no, 2 November 1982, pp 192–9.

Goldsmith, P and Robinson, T *Developing word knowledge* PEN 58 PETA, 1986.

Goodman, K *What's whole in whole language?* Scholastic, 1986.

Goodman, K, Goodman, Y and Hood, W (eds) *The whole language evaluation book* Heinemann, 1989.

* Hudson, C *Spelling: a teacher's guide* Landmark Educational, 1983.

Jenkins, R (ed) *Spelling is forever* ARA, 1986.

Ministry of Education, Victoria *The English language framework* P-10, 1988.

Parry, J and Hornsby, D *Write on: a conference approach to writing* Martin Educational, 1985.

Real literacy shifting the focus Maroondah region publication, 1986.

Rivalland, J 'Teaching spelling: helping the developing speller' in *Australian journal of reading* vol 8, no 1, ARA, 1985.

* Rowe, G and Lomas, B *Spelling for writing* Oxford University Press, 1990.

The teaching of spelling Education Department Of Victoria, 1984.

Turner, P *Spelling in the total language program* PEN 46 PETA, 1984.

Wing Jan, L *Write ways: modelling writing forms* Oxford University Press, 1991.

Children's literature referred to in text:

Cubbin, S *A day in the life of your body* Bookshelf Stage 5, 1988.

Salmon, Michael *Things to do when you are bored* Ashton Scholastic, 1987.

Vaughan, Marcia *Hands* Bookshelf Stage 1, 1986.